BIG FAT PAYCHECK

A Young Person's Guide to Writing for the Movies

COLTON LAWRENCE

BANTAM BOOKS

NEW YORK * TORONTO * LONDON * SYDNEY * AUCKLAND

RL 4.0, AGES 010 AND UP

BIG FAT PAYCHECK

A Bantam Book/May 2004

ISBN: 0-553-37600-4 (trade)
ISBN: 0-553-13122-2 (lib. bdg.)

Visit us on the Web! www.randomhouse.com/teens
Educators and librarians, for a variety of teaching tools, visit us at
www.randomhouse.com/teachers

Published simultaneously in the United States and Canada

Bantam Books is an imprint of Random House Children's Books, a division
of Random House, Inc. BANTAM BOOKS and the rooster colophon are
registered trademarks of Random House, Inc.

PRINTED IN THE UNITED STATES OF AMERICA

BVG   10 9 8 7 6 5 4 3 2 1

BIG
FAT
PAYCHECK

To Shannon, partner in screenwriting crime

CONTENTS

INTRODUCTION

Who wants to be a millionaire?

If you answered, "I do!" this could be the book for you.

As a screenwriter—the person who writes the movies we know and love—you *can* be a millionaire. Some screenwriters become millionaires almost overnight. Some screenwriters never make a dime.

What kind of screenwriter will *you* be?

Becoming a successful screenwriter depends on many things. It helps to know someone in Hollywood; it's even better to have a family member who can get your foot in the door. Becoming a successful screenwriter also depends on luck. If you don't have family connections and don't want to depend on luck alone, the best shot you have at hitting the screenwriting jackpot is writing a kick-butt screenplay.

Big Fat Paycheck: A Young Person's Guide to Writing for the Movies will show you how simple it is to write a script. You, however, will have to supply the kick-butt.

You might think you are not a very good writer. Maybe your spelling sucks and you don't know much about grammar. You will quickly learn that the key part of writing a successful screenplay is the stuff you come up with in your imagination: a dynamic story, exciting characters, and realistic and hip dialogue. Not to downplay the importance of being able to write well, but in screenplays it's more important for you to write in an exciting way than a grammatically correct way.

If you are in your teens or early twenties, you should also be aware that you have a built-in advantage in selling a screenplay. You know what it is?

Your age.

You have something Hollywood wants: youth. As terrible as it sounds, Hollywood looks at you with dollar signs in its eyes.

Movies are a popular form of entertainment, especially for young people. And since you spend so much money at the movies, Hollywood goes to great lengths to make flicks just for you. The wisdom goes like this: young people who fall in love with a movie won't come to the theater just once or twice. A motivated young filmgoer will see a movie three or more times. They are repeat customers. Movie producers *love* repeat customers. Remember *Titanic*? It didn't become the top-grossing movie of all time just because old people liked it. What made *Titanic* so successful was the fact that young people like you (especially teen girls) went to see it half a dozen times or more. Trust me when I say Hollywood goes after you relentlessly to make sure you are at a movie the first night it opens. Then the second night. And the third. And on and on and on.

Hollywood profits off you at the movies (and the video stores) to the tune of *billions* of dollars a year. You are probably their biggest customer. The question is: if Hollywood makes boatloads of money off you, why not turn the game on its head?

Why not make boatloads of money off Hollywood?

There actually was a teenager who made a lot of money writing for Hollywood. She was writing for TV, not movies, but her story provides ample evidence that Hollywood will pay lots of money to a young person who writes in a fresh and professional manner.

This teen sensation's story is somewhat funny, but also somewhat sad for older people. It represents how desperate Hollywood is for a youthful point of view.

Back in the day, there was an eighteen-year-old girl named Riley Weston whom Hollywood branded a wunderkind (which you'll be branded too if you sell your script before the ripe old age of twenty-five) because she could write TV scripts that featured young people just like her who sounded *real*. She signed a fat deal to write for a TV show and received a whopping $300,000. To put that in perspective, Riley banked what it would take you 50,000 hours at a minimum-wage job to earn.

Besides being a highly paid writer, Riley was just like every other teenage girl. She wore baggy jeans and pigtails and painted her nails in polish with names like Cotton-Candy Crunch and Diamond Sparkle. If Riley was similar to the typical young person on *The Real World,* she probably used the word "like" so many times you just wanted to smack her.

Being eighteen and working in Hollywood was probably intimidating. Maybe that's why Riley brought her mom to important industry business meetings with scary people such as agents, managers, lawyers, and TV executives.

Riley even had her own Hollywood office, and it probably smelled of CK One and grape Bubblicious. When not writing about teens, Riley could relax in her sumptuous leather office chair counting her blessings, like not having to work behind a fast-food counter. With her Dr. Martens parked atop her mahogany desk, she daydreamed about the movie premiere she'd be going to later that night. "Ohmygod," she probably wondered, "what am I going to wear?'

Riley's Cinderella story kept getting better and better. With her newfound riches, she splurged on a Miata she could drive like nobody's business—with her mom riding shotgun, of course.

Riley celebrated her nineteenth birthday on the set of

the TV show, where she was now a staff writer. Then the magazine *Entertainment Weekly* dubbed Riley Weston one of the 100 Most Creative People in Hollywood, all 'cause Riley was a teen who could write about other teens.

There was just one problem. Turns out Riley Weston wasn't really a teenager. Riley Weston wasn't even in her twenties. For the love of God, Riley was actually, like, in her thirties!

To make matters worse, Riley Weston wasn't even her real name.

The truth of the matter is that Riley was a struggling actress/writer named Kimberlee, a woman in her thirties who couldn't break into show business. So Kimberlee decided to create Riley Weston, her teenage alter ego.

And Hollywood fell for it! Teen sensation Riley Weston fooled everyone around her. In fact, Hollywood was desperate to believe she existed.

Why?

Because Hollywood wanted to give a boatload of money to a teen writer. Not only would it be good marketing for the TV show, but having a teen on the writing staff would also lend the show authenticity.

So why are we not hearing about more young people making big bucks off Hollywood? An old and bitter screenwriter might say young people aren't mature enough to write a professional screenplay.

Do you feel dissed? I feel dissed for you.

I know you can write a screenplay, and one that is

professional. And despite what some old and bitter screenwriters might tell you, writing like a professional is easier than you think.

You don't need a college education to become a screenwriter. While you need to know the basics of the English language, you don't have to be a genius.

You may become a successful screenwriter at age twelve if you follow the guidelines in this book.

I don't want to oversimplify matters. You will learn to plot a story, develop characters, and write dialogue. You will learn all the basic skills necessary to write a screenplay, and some of the more advanced ones. This information will be given to you in a practical way that is easy to follow.

Writing your screenplay will actually be the easiest and most fun part of the process. And you might not be aware of this yet, but you have to believe me when I say your first screenplay is going to *suck total butt*! It is inevitable, unavoidable, and it is totally okay.

Everyone's first screenplay stinks. I hope that through the rewrite (discussed in depth later) you will be able to salvage yours. Maybe not. It is a chance you must take.

Here is a reality check, and I need to be perfectly honest for a moment. As I said before, writing your screenplay will be relatively easy (much easier than you think). Rewriting your screenplay will be more challenging than writing it, but the rewrite will be very doable if you have patience.

Selling your screenplay, however, will be hard.

Be prepared, because competition in Hollywood is fierce.

Selling screenplays can be very lucrative, but that's exactly what makes it terribly competitive. There are literally thousands of people out there writing screenplays. So it's going to be hard to sell yours, but it *is* totally possible.

This book addresses the hurdles you must jump to write and sell your first script.

It is important to be clear from the beginning about your expectations for your script. Your first script might not ever be salable. Be okay with that. If you can't live with the thought that absolutely nothing could come of your efforts, then don't write a screenplay.

Think about it this way, though: even if your first screenplay isn't good enough to sell, your second one might be. Or your third. Maybe your fourth. Even if you never sell a screenplay, I can guarantee this: you *will* become a better writer. And if you're like me, you will simply enjoy the process of writing a screenplay. You'll enjoy coming up with exciting and unexpected stories, developing new characters, and writing cool dialogue.

All these things are a lot of fun.

I know you, though. You'd rather have the money. Okay, already, let's get you started on writing your screenplay.

Don't forget—you have to supply the kick-butt.

Screenplay and Hollywood Jargon

As you begin reading, you may come across many unfamiliar words. Some of these words, like "slugline," will make no sense. Some, like "agent" or "manager," you might know one meaning of, but they have a particular meaning in screenwriting.

The definition of these words will appear on the page. They represent common screenplay jargon.

Don't feel overwhelmed by the jargon. It will take some time, but soon the meanings of the new words will come easily.

The Purpose of This Book

With the advent of digital technology, there are many young filmmakers out there putting together their first movies. These are called independent films.

This book doesn't necessarily address screenplays meant to be independent films. This book addresses scripts meant to be produced by a big movie studio. You know, Walt Disney Pictures, Twentieth Century Fox, Universal Pictures, Metro-Goldwyn-Mayer (MGM), Warner Bros. Pictures.

You might approach an independent-film screenplay in a different way than is recommended in this book. This book's main purpose is to help a young writer create a commercial screenplay—one that is supposed to make lots and lots of money.

Still, I encourage you to read the book even if you're

trying to write, produce, and/or direct an independent feature film. There are many elements of good storytelling covered in this book. Good storytelling is good storytelling—it doesn't matter if you're writing a big commercial Hollywood movie or an independent film.

SECTION ONE

In the Beginning

CHAPTER 1

Finding Your Voice

In a few hours—the amount of time it will take you to read this book—you will know everything you need to know to write a script. After that, you can call yourself an aspiring screenwriter. Once you write your first script, which will be easier than you think, you can officially call yourself a screenwriter.

Writing a screenplay is something anybody is equipped to do. I am going to be very ruthless in my efforts to unshackle your perception that "It's too hard!" or "I'm not good enough!"

I absolutely *don't* want to hear any whining.

The coolest thing about being an aspiring screenwriter is that it is cheap to get started. To complete your first script, you do not need much in the way of equipment or education; you just need a voice. I'm not talking about your speaking voice; I'm talking about your perspective on the world.

We'll discuss your voice later in the chapter. But if you are reading these words and can make sense of them, you have the skills you need to become a screenwriter. What's more, you've already trained to become a screenwriter and don't even realize it yet. Remember watching a lame movie and thinking, "Who *wrote* this crap?" Well, that was the day you completed your training and became capable of writing a screenplay. You've seen enough movies to know how to write one.

Really, what I am going to do is give you a swift kick in the butt. Anyone can write a script. That includes *you*. And it's not that hard. You'll be amazed at what you already know, and you'll be amazed to learn that it doesn't take that much effort to fill 80 to 120 pages (the standard length of a screenplay).

To become a *high-paid* screenwriter, though, you must write a script Hollywood wants to buy. While your age is a great selling point, Hollywood will still demand that you write a commercial script that can be turned into a movie that millions of people will want to go see at the multiplex.

A Word About Struggling and Professional Screenwriters

You should also know a little bit about your competition. There are tons of struggling screenwriters who know how to write kick-butt screenplays—yet still they can't get writing jobs. Why? They're too old. Bad for them, good for you. They're just not writing the kinds of movies Hollywood thinks will appeal to young people.

You also have something most professional screenwriters

do not have—an "in" with your peers. You know your fellow teens or young adults. You know how they talk, how they act, how they decide to do things, and why they decide to do them.

If you want to compete with both struggling and professional screenwriters, though, you first need to commit yourself to writing like a professional screenwriter.

Practical Advice Instead of Theory

I am writing the kind of book I wanted to read when I first started writing screenplays at nineteen. At that time, I needed a down-to-earth book filled with practical advice from someone who had written but who also remembered what it was like to be nineteen. I didn't need a book that was intimidating.

The only books out there, however, were overly complicated and blathered on and on about "screenwriting theory." Screenwriting theory, by the way, is a boring, backward way of writing. It makes the process too rigid and uncreative. This book is *not* about screenwriting theory. It is a very practical book on writing a script, and it will take you from step one all the way to the end of your first screenplay. If you follow the steps, you will be able to painlessly write your first script.

If I had had this book when I was your age, I think I might have made fewer mistakes. And it might not have taken me such a long time to find my voice.

Okay, so what is this voice stuff all about?

Write What Comes Easiest for Now

I'm sure you've seen tons of movies written by an older person desperately trying to seem hip. Nothing in the flick—situations, relationships, dialogue—represented you or your friends at all.

It is sad but true that when one generation tries to capture the voice of another generation, they rarely do it right. That's not to say that adults can't write movies for teens or young adults and vice versa.

Sure, you might have a script that features a forty-year-old character. You can write that character just fine. Could you write a good script that focuses on a forty-year-old lead character? Probably not. For one thing, you wouldn't want to. Writing about your own age group is probably more exciting than writing about a middle-aged person. For another, it's hard to capture the voice of a generation, particularly when it's not your generation.

When I refer to voice, I mean you should write about the things you're familiar with in the most common language you can use. You are a young person—you should concern yourself with writing about the world as you know it. Write in a simple, clear way that anyone in your age group would understand.

See, right here I'm making things easier for you by telling you this. If you write a screenplay in your own voice, you won't need to use big, fancy words. It's more important to write in a clear and simple way. People in Hollywood who will one day read your script are impatient and overworked . . . and quite a few are not the sharpest pencils in the desk, if you get my drift.

All I am saying about voice stuff is for now, remember your age and write accordingly. This is not to discourage you from writing about things that you are not an expert on. If you are a guy, you can write convincingly about a girl. If you are a girl, you can write convincingly about a guy. You can write about different cultures and religions.

The point for now is that you should write about the things that you feel most comfortable with. Keep your story and your characters (both of which we will discuss more later) within the range of your own experience. That way you will not have to struggle with your first script.

Keep It Simple, Stupid (K.I.S.S.)

When I came to Hollywood as a nineteen-year-old punk, I had a severely deficient maturity level (which, by the way, is only a bit more developed now). My early scripts sounded like they were written by a nineteen-year-old (which was good), but I was not writing professionally (which was not good). Worst of all, I was too ambitious.

My first story, *Burned Legacy*, was about two best friends, a nineteen-year-old white guy and a nineteen-year-old Hispanic guy, and their parents. The biggest flaw in the script was that I did not really know what it meant to be Hispanic. I wrote about a culture I really knew nothing about, and the script sucked total butt.

Do not make my mistake. Do not make your first script too difficult.

For now, your goal is to write a script that will sell. You don't need to be too ambitious with your storytelling. Since you're new to writing, you should K.I.S.S. (KEEP IT SIMPLE, STUPID).

Your young voice is the most valuable thing you have to offer right now as a screenwriter. And through the process of using your voice, you will turn your very important thoughts, feelings, and beliefs into a screenplay. If you write a professional-quality screenplay that captures the voice of your generation, you may very well sell your script and be on your way to making a million dollars.

Two Big Rules You Need to Learn

Before you embark on your quest, we must cover two basic screenwriting rules. Sorry to bring rules up so early in the game, but in screenwriting (just as in life), there are rules you must follow.

The following two rules are discussed in more depth later, but it is important I give you the heads-up about them now.

The fundamental rule is that your script must look a certain way. That's called format. You *can't* break the established rule of how a screenplay must look. If your screenplay doesn't look like all the other scripts out there, you will be called a novice. That means the people in

Hollywood who first look at your script (whom I like to refer to as Big Fancy Hollywood Readers and whom you will learn more about later) will toss your screenplay into the reject pile (meaning the recycling bin).

People in Hollywood, you will learn, look for any excuse to reject your script. If it doesn't look like the thousands of other scripts they have read, you are toast. We'll cover how your screenplay should be formatted in Chapter 4 of this section.

The only other hard and fast rule is that your script *must* have a story. You already know what a story is, even if you do not think you do. Briefly, a story is made of one situation after another. The situation may be mundane: a character talks to a parent at dinner. Alternatively, the situation may be dramatic: a character gets into a car accident.

Your script will have a bunch of situations, and collectively these situations will make up your story. In screenplay jargon, the word for a situation is "scene." A screenplay is a collection of scenes. Here is an example of a scene:

```
INT. THE SCUBA ROOM — DAY


The scuba room is dark and filled with
the RUMBLE of the engine. Joel enters
and sits on a crate. He opens a
magazine and smiles at the images of
```

models in lingerie. At this age, even
fully clothed models will do.

>   PHILIP (O.S.)
>   I see it's time for the
>   father-son talk.

Startled, Joel SCREAMS! Philip pokes
his head through wet suits on hangers.

>   PHILIP
>   Hey, Tiger.

Joel jumps to his feet, embarrassed.

>   JOEL
>   Dad? What are you doing
>   here!

>   PHILIP
>   Aren't you glad to see
>   me?

>   JOEL
>   Uh, yeah. *Yeah!* Not so
>   sure about Mom, though.

                    PHILIP
          I'm hoping she'll
          understand.
               (beat)
          Gotta cancel the Grand
          Canyon, kiddo.

                    JOEL
          That means you got the
          dig in Iraq? *Way* cool!
               (beat)
          Mom's gonna turn the
          boat around when she
          finds out you're on
          board.

                    PHILIP
          That's why we gotta keep
          it a secret till we're
          out to sea. Okay?
               (tousles Joel's hair)
          Go on, before your mom
          comes looking for ya.

     Joel nods, then starts to leave. He
     looks back.

                    JOEL
        I'm really glad you're
        here, Dad.

                    PHILIP
        I miss you, kiddo. Like
        the old days, huh?

Joel grins and exits. Philip turns back
to the place he was hiding and pulls
out a scuba tank — it's marked with a
piece of fluorescent tape. Philip sits
on a stool and twists the top of the
tank, opening the lid. He pulls out a
map, studying it curiously.

That, my friend, is a scene. Your screenplay can have anywhere from 50 to 150 scenes. (There really is no proper number of scenes—it's up to you.)

Why the scene looks the way it does is not as complicated as it might appear. More on the ins and outs of a scene later.

For now, I simply want you to begin thinking of your screenplay as a collection of scenes. If you think about writing one scene at a time rather than writing an entire screenplay, you won't be intimidated about writing your first script.

There, that was simple. More guidelines will follow, but for now, you know the basic rules.

The reason I think it's important not to concern yourself with too many rules right now is this: when people face too many rules, they either ignore them or give up writing because they are frustrated. Essentially, they freak out because they are intimidated.

You will not give up in frustration. You *will* write your screenplay.

No More Excuses

In case you haven't noticed it yet, I am trying to beat this into your head: writing scripts is pretty easy. You will probably suck the first time out, but get over it. How many times did your favorite athlete, actor, singer, writer, or painter suck before they got better? The first time they started doing the things that now look so easy for them, they sucked *big*-time.

I hope by now you are at least committed to starting your first screenplay. And you should start it today. Even if you just write FADE IN: (the standard way most scripts start) on a scrap of paper, it shows commitment on your part to becoming a screenwriter.

It's easy, it's easy, you'll suck, you'll suck, get over yourself, get over yourself, it's fun, it's fun!

Supplies You Will Need

- ✓ A notepad and pens/pencils. (Make sure you get some red pens because they're fun. I'll tell you why later when we talk about rewriting.)
- ✓ A computer. (If you don't have one, you'll need to find access to one.)
- ✓ White printer paper with three holes. (Sold at office supply stores—five hundred sheets go for three to ten bucks.)
- ✓ Brass round-head fasteners, 1¼ inches long. (Sold at most major office supply stores. You stick these "brads" into the three-hole paper. A box of a hundred runs from five to fifteen bucks.)
- ✓ Diskettes, Zip disks, or CDs to back up your computer files. (Back up your scripts and other writing materials *frequently*. The worst day ever is when you lose hours upon hours of the stuff you have written.)

That's about it. You may start your first screenplay with everything listed above.

A few bucks for a potential million-dollar payoff? *Not* a bad return.

CHAPTER 2

Getting into the Write *Frame of Mind*

Consider this your training to become a screenwriter: sit in a chair for a few hours and stare at a computer screen with a blank look on your face.

There—you're a trained screenwriter.

Not really. Screenwriting is a *little* more involved than that.

I've said it before and I'll say it again: writing scripts is pretty easy. Yet I have tricked you. While writing a script is easy, becoming a writer is *not* easy.

You might read this book and get all excited about writing, then start but never finish a script. You might not like being a writer. Writing can be boring. You have to sit in one place for a while. Even if you're lazy and like to sit on your butt all day, writing is still work. It's not like you can totally veg and still finish a screenplay. You will need to engage your mind and do some hard work.

Once you start writing, though, you might find that you enjoy it. You get to come up with really cool ideas. When you write, two hours might pass but it only feels like twenty minutes. And when you review what you've written, you're like, "Where did *that* come from?"

That came from your creativity.

You Are a Creative Being

Most people are more creative than they want to believe. The strange thing is, people use their creativity all day long and don't even realize it.

Creativity comes in many forms. When you daydream or lie in bed at night and think of stuff before you fall asleep, you are being creative.

Becoming a screenwriter is pretty much like being a day/night dreamer. You fantasize about a story and characters and the things that happen along the journey. And if you're lucky, you'll be paid a bunch of money to become lost in those wonderful thoughts.

If you're the type of person who's bursting with ideas—you're creative and you know it—you don't need me to pep-talk you about the beauty of creativity. The following words are mainly directed at those who have a hard time believing in their creativity:

There is no harm in trusting that you are a creative being. Nothing bad will happen to you. We all have access to the same amount of creativity. I do not have any more creativity than you. Stephen King does not have any more creativity than me. The only difference among you, Stephen King, and me is the degree to which we practice using our creativity. I probably have more practice harnessing my creativity than you do. Stephen King has *much* more practice than I do. You, my friend, have an edge, though. As writers age, they have fewer fresh ideas.

You are young and are probably just now starting to tap into your world of ideas, whereas Mr. King and I are slowly running out of fresh ideas.

If you still refuse to believe you are creative, you may have a hard time starting your first script. You may start writing something and then suddenly tear it up or delete it. "This sucks," you say, or, "I'm no good at this."

Relax and chill.

You simply need to jump a hurdle on your way to becoming a screenwriter.

You need to murder something.

Kill the Critic

Now, don't go hunting down a movie critic.

What I mean is you should kill that voice in your head. You know. The one that says, "You can't write! You're not creative enough! Sure, you can string words together— but your writing *sucks*!"

Get rid of those thoughts. You don't need them.

Very soon you will learn the importance of being critical of the things you have written to improve your work. What you never want to do is become critical of *yourself. You* are the vessel to your unique creativity. That means without you, your creativity will not be shared with others. So you're kinda special.

It's particularly important to be nice to yourself because you will not find many allies and mentors on your screenwriting path. Instead, you will find many critics. While some people will help you along your journey as a screenwriter, most people in Hollywood will tell you that your writing is no good.

Someone *must* be in your corner rooting for you.

Sometimes the only one you can depend on is *yourself.* So be nice to yourself about the way you write. Kill that critical part of your mind that finds fault with your writing and your abilities as a writer. You already know everyone writes pure crap in the beginning. The difference between the people who write pure crap (all of us) and the ones who succeed in making money at their craft is this: the writers who make the money realize their script needs a lot of work. They commit themselves and work very hard on their writing.

You need that same commitment.

So let's take the first little step to revealing your talent. It's a fun, if disgusting, step.

You need to vomit.

Yes, you heard it here first. Screenwriting is one big barf on paper.

Throw Up Ideas

After you've acknowledged you are creative and have killed the critic, you need to come up with ideas. These ideas may one day be turned into screenplays.

Throwing up ideas means you're figuring out what you want to write about.

Ideas come in many shapes and sizes. You may get an idea and write three to ten pages without stopping. Or you may get an idea that's just a sentence. Doesn't matter.

To vomit up all these ideas, though, you need to be open to inspiration. Inspiration is something that triggers thoughts or feelings you then turn into ideas.

How do you recognize inspiration? Easy—things that interest or fascinate you provide inspiration. Being open to inspiration means you're on the lookout for cool ideas.

Many Things Trigger Inspiration

When I first started writing, my inspiration came from the people in my life, other movies, books I loved, music, and traveling. The first idea I ever came up with for a movie was actually inspired by a road trip I took with my dad.

I was nineteen and traveling by diesel truck from Los Angeles to Calgary, Canada. My dad and I were transporting Friesian horses that belonged to a ranching family for whom my dad worked. It was the first time I had really traveled outside of Texas or California. The new sensations were very inspiring. I felt very open to this new experience, as if I was seeing the world for the first time. My mind worked overtime.

After a few days in Calgary, I wandered around at an exhibit hall at the horse show and came across a booth promoting little chips that fascinated me. The chips were implanted just under a horse's skin, could store its medical history, and also acted as a tracking device if the horse went missing.

That night in my motel room, I wrote my first screenplay concept, came up with my first title, and wrote a story outline (before I even knew what a story outline was). *The Shelter* was about an artificially intelligent computer C.I.M. (computer intelligence module) that controlled a small bunker underneath a prestigious university.

The "backstory": The bunker or shelter was to be used in the event of nuclear or biochemical attack.

The basic story: A catastrophic event occurred, and eight people made it to the shelter and were locked inside . . . with no way of opening the door.

Everything now was controlled by the C.I.M., which happened to be psychotic due to a glitch in its code.

The eight people in the shelter were each implanted with a device that could track their movements. These devices fed data into the C.I.M.'s database so the computer could tell if the people were diseased, malnourished, or suffering from a minor illness. It could also deliver some nasty surprises—electric shocks or other forms of torture.

There was much more to the story, but the point is that a new experience in my life inspired me to write.

By the way, I never wrote the script. That happens quite frequently with ideas. You get an idea, write like an obsessed person, and then drop it like yesterday's love interest. That's okay. For every fifty story ideas you come up with, only one might become a script. Just remember, to throw up ideas you first need to be open to inspiration. You'll find inspiration in unusual places if you're open to new ideas. Even insignificant things in your life could trigger an idea that may be turned into a screenplay.

Inspiration Is Fascination

If you find fascination with something, there is an idea just waiting to happen.

Nurture your fascination with things. If something interests you, daydream about it. Let your mind wander. Let your interest in a particular topic lead you to an idea.

If you have a hard time identifying fascinating things in your day-to-day life (sometimes life can be *really* boring and predictable), go to the library. Read a new book. Read the newspaper or a magazine. Many stories that become TV movies or feature films are found by writers in newspapers or magazines.

Look at familiar things in your life in a new and exciting way. Many writers like to people-watch in order to find inspiration for ideas. Start imagining the lives of the people you see at the mall or in classes. Why does a certain person dress or behave as he does? Create a twisted backstory for him. Maybe he is an alien or a psycho killer.

Venture outside your comfortable routine and look for new things. If you go online regularly, find a new Web site you would never have thought to visit. See what, if anything, about the site inspires you.

Open the dictionary. You can actually find many ideas for characters or stories. I opened the dictionary the other day and found the words "whorled" and "loosestrife." Those words were very compelling.

With a few modifications, those words became a futuristic character named Whorl Loostrif. He could be a precious-metal miner on a distant planet. I could develop a whole story just around that one interesting character name.

Encyclopedias, obviously, are also good places to turn for inspiration.

Another way to find inspiration for ideas is by listening to music.

Also, take note of your dreams. You'll find that some pretty strange things happen in your head while you sleep. Your dreams may be stories waiting to be written.

Boring People Are Bored

None of the inspiration activities I mentioned should be boring to you. Looking for inspiration is not like homework. There's no need to wade through tons of stuff to find inspiration. If you aren't interested, you're not inspired. So move on.

There's no downside here. You simply avoid the things that don't spark your imagination.

The fun part of writing a script is finding the ideas *you*

want to write about. Ideas will come when you feel inspired. Inspiration comes by simply paying attention to the things that fascinate you.

Once you become inspired by something, ideas may come to you fast and furious. Rather than letting ideas pass you by, you need to write them down.

Capture Your Ideas

As you develop in your quest to become a screenwriter, ideas will pop into your head like firecrackers.

Unlike firecrackers, ideas need to be caught.

Even if your ideas are messy and all over the place, write them down. Write down whatever you are thinking or feeling. Don't analyze (or become critical). Just vomit. There's no way for you to know whether something you write down could be the basis of your first script or become a scene in your movie.

Don't reject ideas. Get them all out. You will need a pool of ideas to work with before you start writing your first script.

Journals Are Not Stupid!

From this moment forward, you need to find a place to jot down your ideas. And ideas don't just come when you are looking for them. Ideas will come when you are at school, in the car, and—grossly enough—on the toilet.

Carry a pad or notebook and pen or pencil with you at *all times* (or most of the time). This will be your screenwriting notebook or journal. Whatever you want to call it, buy one ASAP and dedicate it to screenwriting. Try to have it with you wherever you go. Truthfully, though, you can wait until after your visit with a toilet to write down your idea.

Whenever inspiration leads you to an idea, *write your idea down as fast as humanly possible.* There's nothing worse than forgetting a good idea. Your screenwriting notebook or journal will be the place you write down any number of things. Maybe it's an interesting comment you overhear.

One day at work an elderly man entered an elevator with me. He was an interesting-looking character, with patches of hair on brown liver spots across his scalp. We stopped two floors down, and the elevator doors opened to reveal a Federal Express guy.

The old man was really troubled by the FedEx guy. He squinted because he couldn't see very well and finally tapped the guy on the shoulder.

                    OLD GUY
          Does that logo on your
          shirt say Funeral
          Express?

I never used that particular comment in any of my scripts, I just thought it was peculiar and wrote it down.

The point is, you should write down interesting things

you hear, see, or come up with in your creative mind. You won't use 99.99 percent of the stuff, but that .01 percent could be the idea that leads you to a million bucks.

You Need Access to a Computer

When you're ready to write, you need mental and physical space to develop your ideas. More importantly, you need a computer.

I hope your family has at least one home computer. If not, don't feel bad. I didn't have a computer when I was in high school. My family was dirt poor. Then I got an office job. The people I worked for trusted me enough to give me keys to the workplace. After everyone left for the night, I stayed and wrote on my work computer. There were no distractions. *That* was huge in terms of my development as a writer.

There are many places to find access to a computer. Find one, because you are really going to need it.

You may write your entire screenplay in your notebook or journal. That's totally cool. At some point, though, you must put your screenplay onto a computer. How else will you save, edit, print, or e-mail your work of art? Your script must be put into some sort of fixed file.

I'm Faster than You Are

If you don't know how to use a computer and you don't know how to use a word-processing program like MS Word, then you'd better learn how to use both very quickly. There's another skill you need that I bet even the most technically savvy among you don't have: typing.

You and I are from different generations (I am old, you are not), but there is one thing that hasn't changed over the years, and that is the necessity of learning to type on a keyboard. Verbal typing technology (where you tell the computer what to write) is around, but it's not very practical for screenwriting.

I took a typing class in school. I have no idea why I took that class, but if you want to know the truth, learning to type was the smartest thing I did for my writing career. I don't know if schools offer typing anymore, but if yours does, take it. Like, right now.

Learning to type is like learning a foreign language. It's easier when you're young. Typing requires manual dexterity. It also requires that the two hemispheres of your brain work together. It requires that your fingers keep up with your thoughts. If you think faster than you type, writing becomes extremely frustrating. If you feel confident in your typing ability, writing your screenplay will be much easier. You'll be able to write your ideas as fast as they come to you.

There are software programs that can help you learn to type. If you can afford to spend twenty bucks and want to learn to type more efficiently, buy a program and teach yourself.

The best way to learn to type is by practice. Hopefully you chat and IM enough so that your typing is getting up to speed. If not, do yourself a favor and practice typing—I cannot overstate its importance.

Tell Other People to Back Off

If you have access to a computer and want to start your screenplay, you should make it clear to people you need time to write.

People might not understand and pester you to go out and do something, but you need to be firm. You need to be alone to develop your ideas. When it comes time to start your first script, you need to write without distractions.

Some people won't like it when you start avoiding them to do your creative thing. People may demand that you spend more time with them. Or *else.*

You know what you have to do. Drop 'em.

Okay, not really. Just be firm—you need alone time to work.

Set a Writing Schedule

The difference between people who say they want to write and people who are writers (and cash the fat checks) is that, well, the writers actually *write.* They have discipline and devote a certain amount of their day to their work. Some people decide they will write one scene a day. Others decide to write for two or more hours a day. They work by a schedule. It keeps them focused and it ensures that their screenplays get written.

A schedule doesn't have to be totally inflexible—you have to go with the flow. Some days you may want to write but you have no time. That's cool. The point is that after you find your writing space, you should set a writing schedule so that you devote a certain part of your day, every day, to writing. Whatever makes sense for your daily life.

Just make sure you're not *too* lazy!

You Can Do This!

If you are reading this book, something drew you to writing for the movies. It could be the money, but it could also be that your creativity is looking for an outlet. You probably love movies, wish they were better, and have some ideas of your own.

You should explore those ideas and start writing.

An important thing you need to do right now, before you begin your quest to write a script, is to open your mind completely to these new ideas that will be coming to you. Rather than worry whether an idea is good or bad, your job in the beginning is to move forward. The surest way to stop your progress is to overthink something, to become too critical of yourself, your ideas, or your writing abilities.

Get Out of Your Own Way

There will come a time when you must become very critical of your work. *Trust* me when I say you are going to have to be the *most* critical person in the world with your ideas later in the writing process. But how are you ever going to write your script if you have that critic in your head saying, "Who do you think *you're* fooling?"

You already know you are going to suck the first time out. That should take some of the pressure off. For now, I want you to keep it fast and loose. Open your mind to ideas and inspiration. Take some steps to show you are disciplined enough to become a writer.

Most important, trust that you *can* do this!

CHAPTER 3

Losing Yourself in the Process

In my day, screenwriting books never talked about the actual process of writing. But I think it is very important that you know what to expect.

Writing isn't just about putting pen to paper or typing into a computer. Becoming a writer is a process. Consider this a process similar to being possessed by a demon. Little by little, writing takes you over and—uh-oh—there's no turning back.

It's in your soul.

Creative Mode

When you begin to write, you may become a distant and perhaps even selfish person. Because when you begin a project, something overtakes you. You feel like you are on creative fire. You are on top of the world and completely lost in your imagination.

Your brain is sizzling with creativity.

The time you spend writing is so unique that you forget to do all the normal activities like brushing your teeth, eating, returning a call from the special someone who makes your heart race. In creative mode, you may write for hours, which completely ruins your chance of falling asleep at a decent hour.

Creative mode is wonderful. You feel possessed by a creative energy and have no doubt of your abilities. The critic is dead and everything you are writing is brilliant.

You write and writ . . . and wri . . .

Crash.

Burnout.

Reality Mode

"Lord, my breath stinks. I'm starving. Why is everyone around me looking at me like I am the devil?"

Reality mode brings you back down to the world. You have to reestablish your daily routine and relationships with the people around you.

Staying in creative mode too long has repercussions. Your grades drop. You are fired from your job. Everyone hates the new you.

Don't Forget You Have a Life

Creative mode is great and all, but it is important to remember that you still have a life.

When you begin writing, you may become very excited about your new craft. Just don't forget your boundaries.

You know how much sleep you need to function properly. You know you have to go to school or work. Don't let important relationships suffer because of your writing. Don't let the creative mode consume you. Stay in control of your time, as much as that is possible, and fulfill your obligations to the world.

An interesting thing happens when you start to write, though. You begin to reprioritize things in your life. Perhaps you stop hanging out with a friend who gets you into a lot of trouble. Perhaps you forgo watching some lame sitcom in favor of writing. (Trust me when I say your TV viewing will diminish considerably when you start writing a screenplay.) Due to some of these positive adjustments to your priorities, your parents and/or girlfriend/boyfriend may be thrilled to see you turned on to writing.

Unless, of course, they are the ones who are reprioritized!

I bring all this up just so you know that escaping reality and dealing with reality are two dynamics you will experience when you begin writing. It's totally okay if you get lost in thought when you are writing. It's actually very important. But it's just as important to remember that you have obligations that have nothing to do with writing.

And for God's sake, brush your teeth!

CHAPTER 4

Formatting and Technical Stuff

By now, you should feel confident about your screen-writing abilities. You're motivated (million bucks, million bucks), you know you have an in with Hollywood's biggest target audience, you've seen enough movies to be able to write one, and you're creative.

Okay, so now what?

Now comes the part where you become familiar with what a screenplay looks like.

I should warn you up front that a script is unpleasant to read. I know this because every time I give a screenplay to someone who has never read one, they say, "Can't you make it look more like a book? This format is very unpleasant to read."

Well, in a word, no. Screenplays must look a certain way. That's called format, remember?

Screenplays and Books Look Really Different from Each Other

A screenplay is essentially made up of two things:

descriptive passages and dialogue.

A descriptive passage tells what will be *seen* on the movie screen. It establishes setting, introduces characters, and explains the action.

Dialogue is what the characters say.

Descriptive passages and dialogue pretty much make up each scene of your script. *They are the two most important parts of your screenplay.*

See how simple it is? A screenplay is made up of scenes. Each scene is mostly made up of two things: descriptive passages and dialogue. That's it!

Your challenge as a screenwriter really boils down to this: to become really, *really* good at writing tight, visual descriptive passages, and interesting, realistic dialogue.

Descriptive Passages

Descriptive passages are this simple:

```
Heidi walks through a dark room filled
with books. There's a strange door. She
opens it. Beyond is a huge snake that
lifts itself up, ready to strike. Heidi
slams the door.
```

Notice that it is written in the present tense. That means the script is written as if the action were happening right now.

You wouldn't write it this way:

```
Heidi walked through a dark room filled
with books. There was a strange door.
She opened it.
```

That's how many books are written—in the past tense.

In screenplays, you *always, always, always* write it this way:

```
Heidi walks through a dark room filled
with books. There's a strange door. She
opens it.
```

It's as if it's happening as you read it.

Again, a descriptive passage tells what will be *seen* in the movie screen. A descriptive passage provides descriptions of essential things in the scene and explains the action.

A girl walks through a dark room (action and then a description of the room), sees a door, and opens it (action). Beyond is a huge snake that lifts itself up, ready to strike (description of what the character sees, followed by action). The girl slams the door (action).

Dialogue

As for dialogue, if this were a book and Heidi opened a door and saw a snake, it would be written as follows:

"Holy crap!" Heidi said.

However, in screenplays, you write it like this:

```
                    HEIDI
          Holy crap!
```

The Essence of a Screenplay

To put it all together, a screenplay is mostly made up of descriptive passages and dialogue. Descriptive passages are always written in the present tense.

```
Heidi walks through a dark room filled
with books. There's a strange door. She
opens it. Beyond is a huge snake that
lifts itself up, ready to strike. Heidi
slams the door.

                    HEIDI
          Holy crap!
```

12-Point Courier

You will notice that the example of Heidi and the snake is set in a different typeface than the rest of this book. That's because in scripts, you must always use a font called Courier, and it should measure 12 points. Courier is an ugly font and it's uncreative, but that is the font people in Hollywood expect to see. If you write your script in another font, you will shoot yourself in the foot.

Your screenplay must be typed in this
font. Get used to it.

Where to Find Free Screenplays to Study

It's important for you start reading screenplays to
become familiar with descriptive passages and dialogue.
The Internet is the best place to find free scripts to read.
Here are some places to find scripts:

www.big-fat-paycheck.com—my Web site.

www.script-o-rama.com—one of the most popular sites
of its kind on the Net. Has been around for a long time.

www.zoetrope.com—a Web site we'll talk about later.

If the scripts you come across on the Internet have been
written correctly, they will pretty much all look the same.
As I was researching this book, though, I went online to
find some screenplays and noticed some shocking differ-
ences in the ways various scripts looked. Many beginning
writers don't know the rules of format, or they know the
rules and try to change them.

Do not fall into this trap. Your script should look *very*
simple. People in Hollywood call this a "clean" script. You
want to write a clean script.

A Script Is a Blueprint for a Movie

Filming a movie, if you don't already know this, is a
hugely expensive undertaking. It takes millions and millions of dollars.

Before a movie is a movie, though, it's a screenplay. A

screenplay or script tells a story through words that evoke images. Without your script, there are no images to see. Without your script, there is nothing to be filmed. Without anything to film, there is no movie.

Your script is very important.

Your script is also a creative *and* technical document. It's a blueprint, similar to what architects use to build a house. As a blueprint, your script will be filled with specific instructions. So let's break down a scene and take a closer look at what some of the things on the page actually mean.

Sea Creatures

1. FADE IN:

2. Flashlight scans images carved into a cave wall. 3. PAN the images that show Neanderthal men and women in various stages of activity. The final image: a Neanderthal man fishing.

4. DISSOLVE TO:

Ice. A fish wiggles through a crack torn in a fissure of ice. The fish moves, an upward struggle, fighting its way through the frigid maze.

5. EXT. ARCTIC LANDSCAPE — DAY

Snowstorm. **6.** A NEANDERTHAL MAN wearing bearskin pulls a fish from the ice with his crude fishing line. The Neanderthal man proudly grabs his catch.

The ice beneath the Neanderthal man crumbles and breaks off into the water. The man looks up: a campsite made of huts erected in a circle is lost into freezing sea. **7.** SCREAMS. The TRIBE of Neanderthal men and women scramble as the ice gives way under their feet.

The man drops his fish and it flops onto the ice and makes it back to the water. The man looks up: half his tribe drifts away on a sheet of ice. More SCREAMS. Scared and confused tribe members rush to the edge of the ice sheet, desperate to get off. Slowly they disappear into the torrential snow.

> **8.** WILLIAM (V.O.)
> They were a dying breed
> of man who existed
> during the last Ice Age.

EXT. A FLOATING ICE SHELF — DAY

The Neanderthal tribe floats on a large
sheet of ice. The ocean is littered
with icebergs.

>   WILLIAM (V.O.) (CONT)
>   It was a tribe with many
>   legends. The romanticist
>   in me wants to believe
>   their story of a
>   drifting ice shelf that
>   brought them to this
>   island.

What It All Means

1. <u>Almost every screenplay you write should start with FADE IN</u>.

FADE IN is a term that means the audience stares at a black screen, waiting for the movie to begin. Then something comes onto the screen. We have just "faded in" to the first scene of the movie.

FADE IN is the standard way most screenplays begin.

Your First Descriptive Passage

2. <u>This is your first descriptive passage.</u>

The descriptive passage tells what will be *seen* on the

movie screen. It introduces essential things in the scene and explains the action.

Your descriptive passages should be short, sweet, and visually interesting. More on this in Section Three: How Cute—Your First Script.

Avoid Camera Instructions

3. <u>PAN is a camera instruction.</u>

Camera instructions tell a director what to do with the camera filming the scene. Camera instructions are always capitalized. In this case, PAN means the camera will move in a sweeping motion across images in a continuous flow.

Try not to use camera instructions. They will clutter your script and make it more difficult to read. I probably should have cut PAN out, but I wanted to show you the example.

Transitions

4. <u>DISSOLVE TO is what is called a transition.</u>

DISSOLVE TO specifically means one image on the screen will dissolve into the next image. It is used to imply either time or space between scenes.

CUT TO is another transition, and it is widely overused. It means you jump from one image to the next. CUT TO is unnecessary most of the time. Review screenplays online and notice how many use CUT TO. Try not to overuse this transition. It clutters the script.

Sluglines

5. <u>EXT. ARCTIC LANDSCAPE — DAY is called a scene heading, action line, or slugline. We'll just call it a slugline.</u>

The slugline tells the reader of your script whether the scene takes place inside—INT. for interior—or outside—EXT. for exterior. It tells the reader the location of each scene and what time of day the scene takes place: Dawn. Morning. Day. Dusk. Night.

A slugline goes at the beginning of almost *every* scene.

The observant among you might wonder why I didn't start the script off with a slugline. Technically, it is the beginning of a scene and so it warrants a slugline. My screenwriting partner and I made a stylistic choice not to provide a slugline. We wanted to get into the opening scene as quickly as possible.

Capitalize a Character's Name or Description the First Time They Appear in the Script

6. <u>NEANDERTHAL MAN is a character. Always capitalize a character's name or simple description the first time they appear in the script.</u>

If Neanderthal Man were to appear later in the script, his name would not be written in all capitalized letters in the descriptive passage. He would be referred to as Neanderthal Man.

The reason this character is called NEANDERTHAL MAN and not NED JENNINGS or some other name is that he's not going to be in the story very long. There's no need to name him. Characters we only see for a very short while in a script should get a generic name. SCHOOLTEACHER. GIRL WITH BRACES. POLICE OFFI-CER. These are simple descriptions. The first time they appear in the script, they are capitalized.

Capitalize Sounds

7. <u>SCREAMS is capitalized because sounds in a script are always capitalized.</u>

Anytime there is a sound in your script, it is capitalized. It's silly, but it's what we screenwriters do. Examples: Music BLARES. Gun BLASTS. The plane ZOOMS away.

Capitalize Character Names When They Speak Dialogue

8. <u>Always capitalize a character's name when they speak dialogue.</u>

WILLIAM is a character in the movie and he is speak-ing dialogue, so his name is capitalized. *Anytime* a char-acter speaks dialogue, their name is capitalized.

The (V.O.) next to his name normally wouldn't be next to a character's name. (V.O.) means voice-over. Use V.O. when the voice of a character is heard over a particular scene—but the character is not actually speaking that dialogue *in* the scene. The voice-over provides narration. You probably won't use (V.O.) very often.

Another parenthetical you might put next to a character's name is (O.S.) That means offscreen.

Say you have a scene where a character sits on the toilet in the bathroom. The character is trying to do his or her business and then someone knocks at the door.

```
              MOM (O.S.)
        You've been in there all
        day! Hurry up!
```

You hear Mom, you just don't see her. Because she is offscreen.

The reason (CONT) is next to (V.O.) the second time WILLIAM speaks is because he has more dialogue. So (CONT) means he CONTINUES to speak.

Finally, who is WILLIAM? He hasn't appeared in the movie yet, and now he's talking? This was another stylistic choice my partner and I made. William is important later, so rather than call him SOME OLD GUY, we used his name, which will be revealed later in the story.

This scene from *Sea Creatures* is actually a bit more complicated than most of the scenes in your script will be. I chose this scene to give you some experience with a few of the technical terms that will go into your screenplay.

Just remember that each scene in your movie should be clean, simple, and easy to read. The meat and potatoes of each scene will be the descriptive passage and the dialogue. Occasionally there will be technical things in your scene—transitions, camera directions, parentheticals, etc.

One technical thing that will be in your screenplay a *lot* is the slugline. Let's take a closer look at it.

Keep Sluglines as Simple as Possible

You already know that a screenplay is made up of scenes. Remember, every scene in your script will begin with a slugline (also known as an action line or scene heading).

INT. THE SCUBA ROOM – DAY

That's a slugline.

To recap, the slugline appears at the beginning of each scene and tells whether the scene takes place inside or outside. If it takes place inside, then you write INT. If the scene takes place outside, you write EXT.

Next, you tell your reader the location of the scene. Scuba room. Barnyard. Classroom. Bathroom. Central Park.

Keep your locations as generic as possible. Make sure the slugline doesn't go across a whole page. An example of a bad slugline:

INT. MRS. MERIWEATHER'S FOURTH-GRADE CLASS-ROOM FILLED WITH OBNOXIOUS KIDS – JUST BEFORE THE SCHOOL BELL RINGS

No.

All we need to know is:

INT. CLASSROOM – MORNING

Unless you have a specific purpose, just stick to these times: Dawn. Morning. Day. Dusk. Night.

Overall, don't get too wee-weed up about the slugline.

Once a person becomes skilled at reading a script, they skip right over them. For your purposes, K.I.S.S. with the sluglines.

Screenwriting Software

A screenplay is a very simple document, but as you have probably noticed, it has a lot of funky formatting stuff that makes it difficult to write.

There are many screenwriting software programs on the market. These programs make formatting your screenplay a snap.

Here's where I run into a quandary: I don't think young screenwriters should spend too much money on screen-writing.

I mentioned that I came from a poor family. I think the reason I gravitated toward screenwriting was the fact that it was very cheap to get started. However, screenwriting software can save a lot of time *and* frustration when you start writing your script.

If you have a computer and can load software on it, I fully recommend you scrimp, save, borrow, and beg enough money to buy screenwriting software. It's totally worth the money.

My Web site, www.big-fat-paycheck.com, features screenplay software reviews and information on how to format your script with a word processor.

CHAPTER 5

Before We Begin

I have a little secret for you. Writing isn't the key to success as a writer.

Rewriting is the key to success as a writer.

Let me say it again: rewriting is the key to success as a writer.

You Will *Rewrite—Get Used to That*

Your script will most likely be written five to ten times. This doesn't include just "tweaks" and "polishes." I'm speaking about a major overhaul. Five to ten times.

FIVE TO TEN TIMES!

In this book, you will learn to develop ideas into stories. You will go through several more steps to find your story. Then you will turn the story into a screenplay. The screenplay will then be rewritten and rewritten and rewritten and rewritten. Then rewritten again.

Again . . . and again . . .

You get my point.

Just so you aren't startled during Section Four: The Violent Art of the Rewrite, I wanted to prepare you for the reality of the rewrite.

SECTION TWO

Developing Germs into a Full-Blown Treatment

CHAPTER 1

Getting You to Treatment

Before you write your script, there will be a step-by-step process to follow. This process will help you figure out the story for your script.

Ugh, you say, I have to plan this script *out*?

I don't want writing to seem like a chore, but good planning now will save you from many painful headaches later. Be assured that planning will *not* take away from your creativity. If anything, it will help you make better creative choices.

Trust me when I say you will save yourself months (if not years) of frustration if you follow the advice in this rather long section of the book. (It's the longest because, you got it, it's the most difficult.)

My main goal for now is to introduce you to a very important document you will be writing called a treatment. A treatment is a detailed outline of the story that will become your script.

These are the steps you will follow before you write your treatment:

Step 1: Decide what kind of movie you're going to

write: comedy, drama, horror, action-adventure, etc. These different types of movies are called genres.

Step 2: Find a snappy idea for a movie. We will call this snappy idea a concept.

Step 3: If you don't have one already, you need a title for your screenplay.

So far, not so bad, eh? You probably already know what kind of movie you want to write, have a concept for a movie, and possibly already have a title.

Once you pick your genre and settle on a concept and title:

Step 4: Develop the characters who will be in your script, give them names, and describe them. This step refers to the creation of character sketches (which does not mean drawing them). Sketching in writing means jotting down ideas. These character sketches will not be too long. They will be general notes or ideas about the characters who will be in your movie.

Step 5: Develop your story. To do this you will:
- Sketch your story.
- Write out key moments or events in your script. These moments are called plot points or story beats.
- Continue to sketch your story and fill in story beats until you have a good handle on what your story is about, from beginning to end.
- Write your treatment.

Your treatment can be as short or as long as you wish. Your treatment, though, should describe all (or most) of the scenes in your movie in as much detail as possible.

Writing a treatment before you write the script will help you find your story and force you to pay attention to structure. Structure means that your scenes will all make sense when they are connected together to form the story. One scene leads to another scene, that scene leads to another scene, and that scene leads to another scene. And everything is logical.

That's structure. Structure is important.

Bad Storytellers Have No Structure

Have you ever heard a guy try to tell a joke and fail miserably? He's like, "Um," and, "Oh, I forgot to mention . . . ," and, "This is really funny," and, "Oh, wait, then she said . . ."

He finally gets to the punch line.

You're like, *Huh?*

You probably didn't wait until the punch line to scream, "Dude, I don't care, just shut *up*!" You were irritated because his joke had no structure.

Stories without structure are irritating.

Stories Without Structure Annoy People

Think of structure as the skeleton of your story. Structure keeps a story on track. It provides logic so that your story makes sense to an audience *and* keeps them entertained.

Think of your story structure like this:

Structure in a screenplay is not easy to see. Thus, it's not easy to teach. Structure becomes most apparent when you *don't* see it. A script without structure is one that isn't easy to follow. Things don't make sense. The story is all over the place.

It's messy.

Treatments help ensure you write a screenplay that's properly structured. How? Writing a treatment forces you to think about your story in a logical way.

Logical, however, does not mean boring.

Spice It Up

To understand structure, think about it like this: you get up in the morning, go to school or work, spend six to eight hours doing really monotonous stuff, then you come home, eat dinner, watch TV, and go to bed.

Logical. Makes sense. It's structured (though somewhat boring).

Once you lay down the structure, it's time to become really creative.

Play the What If? Game

Let's pretend your life is the basis of a story. Say you get up and go to school or work.

Who says the day *has* to unfold the way it usually does? This is where your imagination comes into play. This is where you play the "What if?" game.

What if on the way to school you stop at an ATM for some cash? There's a bank robbery. You are held hostage. You escape, but the cops chase you because they think you were involved in the holdup.

What if you try to get to school because you're scared and want to see your girlfriend/boyfriend? In the school parking lot, there's a huge shoot-out. You are caught in the cross fire, all the while trying to prove your innocence. Trying to avoid being dead.

What if after the smoke clears, you are hauled off to jail? However, videotape from the ATM exonerates you from the bank robbery—you were simply the wrong person at the wrong place at the wrong time.

Finally, after a crazy day, you—a day older and a little bit wiser—return home and fall asleep in your bed.

That is an example of creative structure. Logically,

everything makes sense. Unexpected and exciting things happened too.

Creative structure is a way of saying that tons of exciting things happen in your story. *And* the exciting things made sense.

Structure is not as confusing as it may seem. You will naturally develop structure when you plan your script. Writing a treatment will help you find your structure.

With that in mind, it's now (finally!) time to start working on your story . . . and then move on to your first screenplay.

CHAPTER 2

One Step at a Time

When you go to the video store, you're probably most familiar with the New Releases section.

There is this magical but little-known world in the middle of the store filled with older movies divided into categories.

Step 1: Pick Your Genre

Is your movie going to be a comedy? Drama? Horror? Action? Sci-fi/fantasy? These categories are also called genres. The above are the most popular genres, by the way. Genres usually have at least one subgenre. For instance, within the comedy genre there are: gross-out comedies (disgusting but funny movies), romantic comedies (easy on the gross, a dash of funny, heavy on the love), dark comedies (comedies with a bleak view of the world), and so on.

Other possible genres/subgenres you could write: melodrama, thriller, psychological thriller, action-adventure, Western, gangster movie, farce, satire, and more. There's no right or wrong genre/subgenre. You won't be making a mistake if you decide to write one genre (or subgenre) over the other.

People naturally gravitate to a particular genre. You already know what kind of movies you like. Your best guide for choosing your genre is the type of movie you *most* like to watch. Write in the genre that feels most comfortable.

Finding the Right Formula

Have you ever heard this "Boy meets girl, boy loses girl, boy gets girl back." That's the basic formula for a romantic comedy. A boy meets a girl. The boy falls in love with the girl. The boy then loses the girl because of something that happens in the story. Then the boy spends the rest of the story trying to get the girl back.

Nowadays movies seem to go like this: girl meets boy, girl loses boy, girl wins boy back.

You get the idea.

Watch several movies that fall into the same genre (or subgenre) and you will notice that there are similarities. Movies tend to follow a formula. In romantic comedies, for instance, usually there is a best friend who is important to the story. The best friend is part of the formula. Check out romantic comedies and you will see what I mean.

In fact, once you decide on the genre you want to write, rent a few movies in that genre and watch them carefully. Take note of similarities and you will find *that* genre's formula.

Study genres. Even if you choose not to follow a genre's formula, you still get to rent DVDs and spend a lazy Saturday afternoon watching movies while claiming to be doing research.

Pull Out Your Screenwriting Journal

I hope that by now your screenwriting journal is filled with cool ideas that could be part of your first screenplay. It's now time to sift through all the ideas and pick that special one that will become the basis of your first script. In the screenwriting world, this idea could be called a germ (as in the germ or beginning of an idea), a premise, or a concept. From now on, I'm going to refer to the idea, germ, or premise for your script as a concept.

Step 2: Developing Your Concept

A concept for a movie is usually about someone, a character, and the character goes through or after something interesting. A concept is *not* a scene from the movie you want to write.

A friend once told me he had a concept for a movie. It involved a guy and a girl who meet on the subway and fall in love right there on public transportation. My friend said the movie would be sexy and the music would be incredible and the lighting would be stunning and the girl would be wearing this nice little black dress.

I'm like, "Well, what's your movie about?"

He couldn't tell me. He just had that one scene.

Concepts Should Be Short and Sweet

A concept for a movie must provide the overall idea of your movie. In addition, it should be brief. You will create an entire script from one little concept, so you had better make sure it's a *good* concept.

Okay, so you're probably asking yourself, "How the heck am I supposed to know if I have a good concept?"

Glad you asked.

What Is a High Concept?

A high concept is a concept so exciting and appealing that in just a few words, you know everything you need to know about the story. You immediately *get* it.

Examples of high concepts:

Cats want to take over the world and dogs must stop them.

A whole family forgets a girl's sixteenth birthday.

A detective must keep a bus from going below fifty miles per hour or everyone on board is blown up.

A boy is left home alone on Christmas.

A man transforms himself into a female English nanny to spend more time with his kids.

An undercover detective takes part in illegal drag races in a heavily populated city.

High concepts may be explained in one or two sentences. The person hearing the concept immediately understands what the movie will be about. And it sounds fun and/or exciting.

Stories don't *have* to be high-concept. The main thing you should strive for is to make your concept clean, clear, and interesting.

Concepts should definitely not be stupid or boring.

Concepts Are Important When Trying to Sell Your Script

Having a great concept will make your job much easier when it comes time to sell your script.

Does it seem strange that you need to worry about selling your script *before* it is even written? It shouldn't.

What happens when you spend all your time on a script and no one in Hollywood wants to read it?

That would really suck.

Hollywood won't want to read your script unless they like your concept.

It's as simple as that.

Sparkle, Concept, Sparkle

To figure out if you are working with the right concept for a movie, it's helpful to evaluate and brainstorm your concept.

Evaluating a concept requires flicking the greedy money switch in your head. Is this a concept that has the potential to bank you a million dollars?

If you discover your concept needs more oomph, brainstorm ways to improve it. Brainstorming is a flurry of mental activity. The goal of brainstorming is to develop a concept that sparkles. You evaluate and brainstorm your concept by asking yourself the following questions:

1) Is this concept about someone? And are they going through or do they want something interesting?

You're not looking for too many details in your concept. Just be clear that it's about someone or something and they are going through or want something.

<u>Brainstorm:</u> Who will my story be about, what are they going through, and what do they want? How can I make what the character is going through sound more interesting?

2) Who is my target audience?

The smaller your target audience, the smaller the chance your script will sell. If your concept has strong appeal to young people—guys and girls—you're better off than if it appeals mainly to older people.

<u>Brainstorm:</u> How can I make this concept more appealing to a broader audience without losing what I want to say?

3) Is this concept commercial?

Saying a move is commercial in Hollywood is the same as saying millions of people would go to see it. This question is similar to number 2 but a bit different. Is your concept too personal, something that maybe you and your friends like but really won't appeal to anyone else? Be honest with yourself. If you want to sell your script, it must appeal to millions of people.

<u>Brainstorm:</u> How can I make this concept more popular? (NOTE: This could be when you do one of two things:

scrap the original concept and find something else to work on, or say to heck with it and decide it's the concept for your movie and you don't care if millions of people want to see it.)

4) Does this concept have a hook?

A hook is a thing that sticks in your head. It's catchy. Even if it's not your mom's kind of movie, she should listen to your concept and say, "Wow, that sounds amazing!"

<u>Brainstorm:</u> What angle can I add to make this idea more interesting? Can I make it more high-concept?

5) Is the concept interesting but simple?

If your concept requires a lot of explanation before people get it, you might have a hard time selling your script—even to your best friend!

<u>Brainstorm:</u> How can I explain this concept in a sentence or two so that people will get it?

A Bad Concept Gone Good

Let's take a bad concept and see if I can make it better by evaluating and brainstorming it.

Concept:

A sixteen-year-old girl is spurned by the football jock she loves, so she spends a miserable year in school trying to win him from the head cheerleader.

Um, okay. What's wrong with a concept like that? Does it sparkle?

It's duller than dirt!

Let's analyze it.

This concept is about someone (the girl) and she wants something. Nevertheless, what she wants is not interesting. Simple as that. The target audience for a movie like this is usually one person—the person writing it! It would most likely be intended for an audience of teen girls (a good audience to target). It would probably never be made into a film, though, because it has no hook for teen guys. The concept is too narrow in focus.

Is this concept commercial? Nope. It's too vague. I wouldn't care about the girl and what she wants. The story sounds boring. The concept has nothing catchy about it. If I ever read a concept like that, I would forget about it the minute I finished reading.

The concept could possibly be turned into a high concept with some work. That would require finding a hook. What fabulous, interesting thing could a girl do to snag a guy?

The original concept, though, is clichéd. A football jock? Couldn't he be something more interesting? *Anything* to make the concept snazzier?

The bottom line is that the concept as written is simple, but it is not interesting.

To fix the concept, I need to brainstorm and see if there is any way to improve it.

Here's the original concept:

A sixteen-year-old girl is spurned by a football jock she loves, and she spends a miserable year in school trying to win him from the head cheerleader.

First off, I need to make the concept about someone, not some generic sixteen-year-old. Her name is Kyra Jenson. Her name and age might not be relevant to the concept I ultimately come up with, but it's important that I know a little about her. I need to spend some time thinking about Kyra. I know she's a junior in high school. She wants a guy—I will name him Eric Smalley. Kyra is trying to steal Eric from the head cheerleader, Janie Emerson.

Instead of a football player (way overdone), I'm going to make Eric Smalley a very good-looking but high-functioning autistic guy who, while able to attend school and appear normal, has special needs. He is dating Janie, the head cheerleader, but it's a secret relationship. Eric is able to cover his condition as long as he isn't under pressure. Janie has a huge internal conflict about being in love with a guy others perceive as damaged goods. So their love is kept a secret.

Kyra, an outsider who has a disdain for people who try to fit in, has a strange attraction to Eric Smalley. He seems nervous and awkward, which Kyra finds very endearing. She hates the fact that she can't get close to him. She knows there is something different about Eric, but she doesn't know the full extent of his condition. Eric doesn't socialize with anyone in any way.

Somehow Kyra finds out about Eric and Janie's secret. She thinks Janie is using Eric and he's too gullible to realize how sick their relationship is. She hatches a dramatic scheme to expose the couple, and soon everyone knows the truth about Eric's condition. The funny thing is . . . no one *really* cares. High schoolers aren't as shallow as Kyra, Eric, and Janie thought! Eric is accepted for who he is, and Janie feels foolish for hiding the relationship to begin with.

Kyra is revealed to be an empty and malignant fraud. Not only does she lose her shot at ever snagging Eric, but even her own friends think she *way* crossed the line. Kyra is ostracized from everyone in her school. She sinks lower and lower into depression. Finally, Kyra decides to redeem herself and sets out to correct the damage her actions have caused to her reputation.

So what would be the new and improved concept that is short and simple—that sparkles?

Kyra Jenson seeks a damaged boy to love, but he's involved in a secret relationship with a cheerleader. Kyra exposes the relationship only to find true love has a bite.

Nope, too unwieldy. How about this:

A schoolgirl learns that sabotaging true love for selfish needs can be the most damaging lesson romance ever teaches.

Call it *Pierced* and turn it into a horror movie and you would get requests from Hollywood to read your script.

Concepts Force You to Think About Your Story and Characters

It will take you a while to write concepts that sparkle.

But thinking about your concepts before you write your script will help you figure out if the story you're about to tell needs to be more focused and more compelling.

You've also probably figured out that we've been doing a lot more work than just developing your concept. By trying to improve your concept, you naturally begin to develop your story and characters.

Spend quality time with your concept. Evaluate and brainstorm it. Make sure it's good because you *really* don't want to write a script with a concept no one but you finds interesting.

Step 3: Pick a Title if You Don't Have One Already

Getting back to the concept I titled *Pierced*. That's a good title, eh? Could mean pierced as in lips, tongues, or bellies. Could mean a pierced heart. If it's a horror movie, it could refer to body parts that are pierced . . . and not in an aesthetically pleasing way!

Whatever the concept of your movie, it is important to give it a title. That will make working on the story more real for you.

Your title may change as you start working on your story. At least for now, commit to something.

Blurt out your title.

Come on, no one's listening.

To get ideas for your title, think about movies you like and ponder whether you think they have good titles. If so, what makes it a good title? If not, why does it suck?

Your title should be relevant to the story you want to tell and should be appealing to others. Other than that, it's totally up to you.

Step 4: Character Sketches

Once you find the right concept for your movie, it's time to start thinking about the people who will be in your movie. These are your characters.

Here's a dilemma: how the heck do you know which characters will be in your movie if you haven't even written the treatment?

Here's a tip: you already know many of them. You probably have tons of characters flooding through your head. Now is your time to start sketching them out. Again, by sketching I do not mean draw them (although if you are artistic like that, it's certainly okay). Jot down ideas about the characters who *may* appear in your movie. Their names, their ages, and some general characteristics.

You could do something like this:

Christopher Peet, 21, young and impressionable, good-looking but insecure. Hasn't developed a sense of self and is always fumbling, tripping, or stuttering. Relaxed, he shines. Uncomfortable, he fidgets. Intelligent and honest but naïve.

Amy Jenkins, 24, a recent graduate from college who is looking for the next phase of her life. She's smart and outgoing, but there's something dark in her past that makes her try too hard to be the life of the party.

You may also give your characters a detailed history. This is called a backstory. Writing a backstory for your character means coming up with information about their history that may never appear in your script but that helps you understand your character better.

Some screenwriting books say you should write a detailed backstory for your characters. These books say you should know your characters' favorite color, favorite cereal, most painful memory . . .

Some people find it helpful to write the backstory. I personally think characters come to life when you write their story. My most successful character (the first character I ever wrote that made me money for writing) unfolded as I wrote her. I didn't know a thing about her other than she talked fast and ended her sentences with smiley faces. I knew her name and I knew her age, but that was about it. She unfolded beautifully. Most characters will unfold beautifully if you give them a chance to be real.

There is no right or wrong way to write a character sketch. Write as many details as you like about your characters. The character sketches are for you—to help you get to know your characters better.

Is there a villain in your movie? A villain is also known as an antagonist. Is there a kid sister? A teacher? A parent? A Hollywood movie star? All characters you might want in your movie should be given a quick sketch. You may decide later that some characters don't fit into your story. Or you may find that a couple of characters in your script could be combined into one character. For now, just write about the characters who *might* be in your movie. They may never actually appear, but you don't know that now.

The main things you need to know about your characters for now are their names, ages, and a brief description.

Step 5: Develop Your Story

I would like us all to join hands and say a little prayer. You are going to need it.

You are about to develop the story that will one day be your first script.

To develop your story means you work on it piece by piece until the story reveals itself. This may also be called plotting a story.

There is another phrase you might hear in relation to screenwriting: "story line." Story, plot, story line, and storytelling are essentially the same things.

Gradually you will flesh out your story and figure out what your plot or story is about.

When it comes time to turn their concepts into a story, some people freak out. "Oh my God, there's like so much stuff that goes into a story and I have no idea what to do. . . ."

Smack! That usually brings them back to reality.

There's no reason to freak out. Yes, a story might be a big thing. And if you try to tackle a story all at once, yes, you will freak out.

Developing your story is actually very easy. You just need to follow a step-by-step process.

Remember, a screenplay is made up of scenes.

Your screenplay will have anywhere from 50 to 150 scenes (could be less, could be more).

Your screenplay will be anywhere from 80 to 120 pages long.

Do the math. A 100-page movie with 50 scenes will have approximately how many scenes?

Duh, I just gave you the answer: 50.

So What Else Do We Know About Scenes?

Scenes are the building blocks of a screenplay. Each scene takes place in one location. You know that because each scene starts with a slugline. A slugline is warranted whenever you start with a new location.

Ya with me?

So you don't just start writing a story or a screenplay. You build it scene by scene.

When you start developing your story, you must think in terms of scenes: this scene leads to that scene leads to that scene leads to that scene. If you develop and write scenes, completing your script will be much easier than if you just jump in and try to write the whole thing at once.

How to Find Your Story

If you have a concept and title for your movie but you aren't yet sure how to find your story, there are tricks that will help you.

Know where your story begins and know where your story ends up.

What is the first *big* thing or event that happens in your story? The first big thing or event in your script is called an inciting incident. An inciting incident is a big event in the life of the main character in your story (also known as the protagonist) that sets his or her journey in motion.

Here's an example of an inciting incident:

A guy is dumped by his girlfriend.

Get the Ball Rolling

Start plotting your story by figuring out the inciting incident. That should lead to what your story is *really* about.

Let's take the example of the guy being dumped by his girlfriend. What could happen next? Well, it depends on what you've come up with as your concept.

Let's say the protagonist is named Johnny. He wants to become the youngest astronaut to go into space. The breakup, Johnny's inciting incident, leads him to pursue the dream of becoming an astronaut. The inciting incident is something that happens to the protagonist, in this case Johnny, and it gets the story moving.

The inciting incident, by the way, isn't necessarily the first scene in your movie. There may be a couple of scenes that lead up to it. You want the inciting incident to happen early on in your story, though, say in the first ten pages of the script.

Once you decide on the inciting incident, the second best way to plot your story is to figure out how the story ends.

Every Journey Must End

The way a story ends is called a climax. The climax is the big finale of your movie.

It shouldn't seem strange to think about the end of your movie before you've even written it. You know instinctively how it will end: with a bang. Either your lead character gets what they want . . . or they don't.

Your story leads up to the climax, and then your characters' journey (particularly your protagonist's journey) is over.

Does everyone live happily ever after? Does everyone die?

Something to remember: just as a few scenes might lead to your inciting incident, a few scenes might follow your climax. The few scenes after the climax would be used to tie up loose ends. Those few scenes would be the resolution. Then the story is *really* over.

Know Where to Start and Where to End

You might be the type of writer who knows where you want the story to start but isn't very interested in planning where the story ends. You're leaving your fate up to chance and will go wherever the winds take you. . . .

Okay, Pocahontas, you need to consider that you could be mugged by bad ideas and awful creative decisions.

Figuring out your inciting incident and climax will make it much easier to figure out the scenes that go in between. Trust me on this. So once you know your inciting incident and climax, it's time to assemble your story outline.

A story outline is just what it sounds like: an outline of your story. To write a story outline, you simply jot down ideas about the scenes that will be in your movie.

To get started on your story outline, write out general notes about your inciting incident and your climax.

- Philip O'Connor and his ex-wife are abducted from the family boat by evil Uncle Nick. The kids are left on board the burning, sinking boat.
- Philip and family escape the evil Uncle Nick, who is killed by sharks.

The example is the beginning of a story outline for *Sea Creatures*. It describes the inciting incident and climax.

When I write story outlines, I like to use bullet points. You may write your story outline however you choose. A story outline is for you and you alone. You're writing it to help you figure out what your story is about.

Once you know your inciting incident and climax, begin filling in the stuff that happens in between.

Between the Beginning and the End . . . Is the Middle

Once you know your inciting incident and your climax, you have a good idea that your story has major stretching to do to get from the beginning to the end.

Of course, your story needs a middle. Many screenwriting books will tell you over and over that in order for your script to be successful, it will need a beginning, middle and end.

Well, *duuuuh!* I challenge you to write a story that doesn't have a beginning, middle, and end. It's the nature of a movie: the lights go down; after twenty minutes of ads and coming attractions, the movie comes on (beginning), something happens (the middle), and then the movie ends (the end).

That ain't rocket science.

The middle of your story will be the things that happen between the inciting incident and the climax. You might think that since the beginning and end of your movie will be super-exciting, you can calm things down in the middle.

You would be dead wrong.

Many writers forget a very simple thing: exciting stuff *must* continue happening throughout the story. For a story to keep an audience entertained, the audience must be involved with what is happening. You can't give the audience one good scene and then leave them waiting for thirty minutes before something else exciting happens.

By good, I don't mean full of action. Action movies with lots of explosions can be the most boring movies *ever*. Interesting movies are about movement. Things happen. The story evolves.

So you need to find the middle of your story. What happens in the middle should be as exciting as the inciting incident and the climax.

Here's what I'd like you to do.

Imagine you're in a theater watching *your* movie. Imagine you're seeing the scene that is your inciting incident. Jump forward fifteen minutes.

What exciting thing is happening?

Come on. Create an exciting idea for a scene in your head. What's happening? Write it down.

Then jump ahead fifteen more minutes.

What exciting thing is happening?

Keep doing this until you get to the climax.

Start Thinking of Your Script in Fifteen-Minute Increments

For your story outline, I want you to start with your inciting incident. Then I want you to come up with six exciting events that will happen in your script. These six things will lead to the climax.

Let's go back to the guy who wants to be the world's youngest astronaut.

Inciting incident: Johnny's girlfriend breaks up with him.

Exciting things that happen in the middle of the story:

1) Johnny tries out to become an astronaut and is ridiculed. No one thinks he can do it.
2) Johnny discovers that his evil astronaut dad has hijacked a space station and is demanding money or he will blow it up. Johnny realizes he is the only one who can stop his dad.
3) Johnny undergoes rigorous training to become an astronaut, but he breaks down emotionally, fearing he isn't capable of fulfilling his mission/dream.
4) Johnny has a special moment with the one person in his life—his ex-girlfriend—who can make him believe he's capable of fulfilling his mission.
5) Johnny goes into space and fights his way onto the space station.
6) Johnny realizes his girlfriend was a spy working with his dad all along.

Climax: Johnny confronts his father and there is a huge battle. He kills Dad and sends his girlfriend floating off into space.

By coming up with your inciting incident and your climax, then filling in six major plot points in between, you are essentially guaranteeing that your movie starts off with a bang, has a bang every fifteen minutes, and ends with a bang.

(A note of caution: an idea about a young guy becoming an astronaut would take a lot of research to ensure that it is believable. Remember to choose a story that you feel comfortable writing. If you don't have any clue whatsoever how to make a story like that seem believable, then choose something you feel more comfortable writing.)

Try to fill in what happens in your story every fifteen pages after the inciting incident. Make these plot points as exciting as possible. Continue this exercise until you reach the climax.

And you're not married to your inciting incident, six plot points, or climax, by the way. These things may change as you develop your story. But you need something to work with.

Fill In the Blanks

You should now work on your story outline until you have eight major beats: the inciting incident, six exciting things that happen in the middle of your movie (one every fifteen minutes), and the climax.

Once you accomplish that goal, it is time to go back through your story outline and try to figure out what happens between the eight plot points.

What happens between the inciting incident and your first plot point? It should be exciting, but it doesn't have to be as exciting as the six major plot points. What happens between your second plot point and third? Keep going until you fill all the major plot points.

Once you finish the exercise, you should have an inciting incident, thirteen plot points, and your climax.

You now have fifteen plot points (including the inciting incident and climax).

Add Some Color

Once you find fifteen plot points for your story, you should come up with *new* plot points to go in between them.

Instead of worrying about big events, think of these plot points as color. We will call these color plot points.

Add some color to your story. What interesting things could happen to your characters? Maybe these color plot points aren't about the main story you have been plotting out. The color plot points could be about a subplot.

We will get to subplots in a second, but let me state this: Johnny and his goal to become an astronaut—that's the main story. Johnny's stories with his ex-girlfriend and dad—those are subplots.

For the color plot points, try to be creative and come up with fun ideas that will tie in nicely with the fifteen plot points you already have.

Adding color to your story outline might be tricky since you still haven't fully developed your story. You are only working with plot points right now. So it might be difficult thinking of new things to add. But spend some time on this and try to fill in a color plot point between each pair of major plot points. If you are successful, you will have twenty-nine plot points in all.

Not bad.

And you know what you've done?

You've come up with ideas for at *least* twenty-nine scenes. And probably much more. Because each plot point will probably have to be told in a couple of scenes for it to make sense. And there will probably be a few scenes before the inciting incident and a few scenes after the climax.

See? Creating a story won't be very difficult. Just cut it up into manageable chunks that you can chew.

Of course, you can modify the technique. If you can't think of twenty-nine plot points or a major story beat for every fifteen-minute interval of your movie, that's okay.

Come up with as much as you can for now. As you develop your story, new ideas will come to you. The story will grow and change.

Writing your outline is simply a matter of figuring out your inciting incident and your climax and filling in the plot points between the beginning and end of your story. Once you jot down those beats, you'll have a basic idea of what your story is about.

Plot Points Turn into Scenes

A movie isn't filled with plot points, is it? No, a movie is filled with scenes.

You might find it helpful to think of the twenty-nine (or so) plot points you've come up with as scenes. Because each of the plot points will be the basis of a scene.

Now I want you to think about your story logically. Does one scene lead to the next? Or are there holes in your story? Do you need more scenes to explain to the audience what is happening in your story?

If a scene does not connect with the scene that follows it in a logical way, ask yourself, "What needs to happen in the story to get to the next scene?" Spend time fleshing out the scenes in your story so they connect with each other. What that means is you may need to create more scenes (or plot points) to fill in the blanks. Or you may need to refocus an existing scene (or plot point) and rewrite it so that it connects better with the scene that follows it.

Your ultimate goal with the story outline is to come up with a brief description of the scenes that will be in your movie.

Take a Break

Once you have a solid story outline with ideas for all or most of the scenes that will be in your movie, let the story simmer for a while. Take a few days off. Then come back to the story outline and think about your scenes logically.

Does everything make sense? Are there any holes in the plot? Are you missing some scenes? Do you need a few scenes in the beginning to set up the inciting incident? Do you need a scene or two after the climax to tie up loose ends?

You want to have a general idea about every scene that will be in your story.

Spend as much time as you need to find the logic and completeness of your story.

Screenwriter's To-Do List

- Jot ideas in a screenwriting journal.
- Find ideas and develop them into concepts.
- Evaluate concepts and strengthen them.
- Write character sketches.
- Jot down story beats and create a story outline.
- Work on the beats until the story emerges.

It's Time for Treatment

Once you figure out all (or almost all) the scenes that will be in your movie, the final step before you write the script is to write a treatment. Before you get to the treatment, though, it's important to learn a bit more about stories and the characters who inhabit them.

CHAPTER 3

Once upon a Time

I would love to tell you that there are certain things your screenplay must have for it to work. I can't. If there were a formula for writing successful scripts, everyone would become millionaires by writing them.

Your movie won't necessarily have to have a likable lead character (also known as the protagonist). I've seen some movies where I didn't really like the lead character, but at least they were very interesting.

Your lead character doesn't necessarily need a goal (though goals certainly help, which we will discuss later). The lead character could wander from scene to scene with no direction. Again, the character just has to be interesting.

While your script doesn't need a villain (also known as an antagonist), there must be interesting characters in your story other than the lead character.

Kind of getting the *interesting* thing?

There are some guidelines you can follow that can definitely help you write the best screenplay you are capable of.

Descriptive Passages and Dialogue = Story and Characters

You know that your script will mostly be made up of two things: descriptive passages and dialogue. There are two things you need to work on before writing descriptive passages or dialogue: your story and your characters.

You usually write out your story first (as you are doing with your story outline) and develop your characters later. The reason for this is simple: you need to create a world where characters can actually exist. You have to give them things to do, which you accomplish by creating a story.

So story is more important than characters, right?

Not even.

Don't think for a moment that your characters are pawns in a chess game. A weird thing happens when you start writing your script. Your characters get a life (and mind) of their own. It sounds strange, but it's true. Characters will take over your story—the story you so carefully plotted out. Where you thought you wanted to go in one direction with a story, a character might take you to another place completely.

That's the fun part of writing. The unexpected. The creation of a kick-butt character who comes roaring to life.

Stories usually *do* come first, though, and while they are no more important than characters, we will discuss them first.

Stories Are Interesting. Period.

What do all the movies you have seen have in common?

About the only thing you can come up with, I bet, is that something happens.

A story is an unfolding of events. One scene leads to the next, and that leads to the next.

Is there a science to storytelling? Nope. The best stories are the ones that keep you interested. It's as simple as that.

There are many theories about what makes a good story. There are book writers out there who have made *tons* of money by making screenwriting look like a science. The books develop confusing concepts like Paradigms and Acts and Act Breaks and Reversals and blah-de-blah, blah, blah.

When I first started developing stories into scripts, I wrote what I wanted. Then I picked up a screenwriting book and it said the lead character must have a major life-changing event by page thirty. And I'm like, "Oh, crap. I had some major event happen, but it was on page twenty!"

Over time I've realized it's not a big deal to worry about where life-changing events are placed in a story. The best stories are the ones where interesting things keep happening.

There are two simple things that *are* important to story telling that you should be aware of. I call them economy and recycling.

Storytelling on a Budget

With scripts, you only have 80 to 120 pages to tell your

story. It might seem like a lot, but really, it isn't. Telling your story economically means you only put stuff in your script that *absolutely* needs to be there. And this stuff moves your story forward.

A story moves forward when one thing happens, and it leads to the next thing, then the next thing, and then the next thing . . . until you reach the climax of your story. Simple, right?

Not always. Remember the concept of color? Interesting things that happen in your characters or in your story? Color is important—it's the fun and funky stuff in your script that most likely reveals something interesting about a character. Yet this color *must* be tied to the story. You can't have scenes in your movie that don't have a purpose. Things in your script unrelated to your story will stop your story cold. When you develop your story, do so economically. Each scene in your movie *must* have a purpose. The purpose is to reveal something about your character that's important to your story and/or to propel your story forward. If a scene doesn't move your story closer to the climax, it needs to be cut or refocused.

Okay, big sigh. Let all the negative energy out.

Now go through your story outline and look to make sure each scene actually has a purpose. If you have a scene that is color for color's sake (meaning it's fun but doesn't really fit into your story), you need to turn it into one that moves the story along. Because you just don't have time for unnecessary scenes.

But wait! Maybe that unnecessary scene in your story isn't so unnecessary after all!

Maybe it just needs to be recycled.

A Word About Subplots

One of my favorite old movies is a foreign flick called *Women on the Verge of a Nervous Breakdown*. The movie is about a woman going through one of the most difficult days of her life. In this high-energy story, the lead character races around Madrid by getting into one taxi after another.

Getting into and out of a taxi is not very exciting. But logically, the audience needs to know how the lead character gets from place to place.

To fix a potential problem—having a woman get into one taxi after another—the writer did something creative. He turned the cab rides into a subplot.

A subplot is a story within a story.

Usually you will have a main story, where your lead character (the protagonist) embarks on a journey to fulfill a goal. There are also smaller stories that are relevant to the main plot, but they aren't as important as the main story. These are your subplots.

Subplots are all about recycling. Specifically, subplots recycle story elements. Recycling will help you tell your story economically.

Each time the woman got into a taxi she had the same driver. In a city as big as Madrid, this woman keeps getting the same taxi? It was highly coincidental. But the writer made that part of the story. The cabdriver thinks running into the woman must be fate! And the woman comes to trust the cabdriver and tells him about the crazy things happening in her life that day.

The cabdriver is a colorful addition to the story. The fact that he always seems to show up when the "damsel in distress" needs a ride becomes a very small part of the movie—a subplot—but it works really well.

Beginning, Middle, End

Like story plots, subplots should have a beginning, middle, and end.

Making sure your plots and subplots have a beginning, middle, and end will help ensure that you write your story economically. Getting back to *Women on the Verge of a Nervous Breakdown,* the lead character interacts with the cabdriver once (beginning), sees him again (middle), and then sees him one last time (end).

There are also many other subplots that are masterfully woven into the story.

Since we are talking about beginnings, middles, and ends, let's talk about the power of threes.

1) Beginning. 2) Middle. 3) End.

This isn't exactly scientific, but I wanted to use the power of threes to illustrate a cool and very effective storytelling technique.

Let's say you have a character in your movie who isn't a huge part of the story. He or she only appears once. If he or she is important enough to be in your movie *once,* maybe you should bring him or her back a second and third time.

Johnny and His Mommy

Let's go back to the example of Johnny, the wannabe astronaut. Let's say Johnny hates his mommy. She abandoned him when he was very young.

Before he leaves for astronaut camp, Johnny wants to give her a piece of his mind. He finds out where she lives and goes to her house but can't bring himself to knock on the door. He watches Mommy and her picture-perfect family through the front window.

That's the first time Mommy appears in the movie. You might think that's enough—you don't need to bring her back. Mothers are important, though. Johnny's mommy is obviously important to him. Why not add some power to your story and bring Mommy back? A second time (middle). And then a third time (end).

You don't have to do this with every character in your story. Important characters, though, can be brought back. You *did* put them in your story for a reason. So consider whether certain characters should reappear somewhere later in your story.

This is also called setup and payoff. Setup and payoff applies to all important things in your story (not just characters or subplots).

To explain setup and payoff, let's use a tennis analogy. You are about to serve. You throw your tennis ball up into the air (setup), it flies up and comes back down (middle), and then you whack the crap out of it (payoff).

If you set up something important in your story (Johnny misses his mommy), the audience will naturally want to know what happens. If you never bring Mommy up again, the audience will be like, "How sad, Johnny never got to make amends with his mommy!" Don't leave the audience hanging. If you set up something important in your movie, the audience will expect you to show how it is resolved. (Resolution is another way of saying payoff, by the way.) You should always try to resolve or pay off important things that have been set up in your movie.

Setups and payoffs don't always have to be important things, though, nor do they have to be done in threes. For instance, in *Women on the Verge of a Nervous Breakdown*, the first time the woman meets the taxi driver, she is crying and asks for eyedrops. The driver, who has the car stocked with every other amenity, berates himself for not thinking of stocking his cab with eyedrops.

Later in the movie, the woman receives a faceful of a tomato drink that burns her eyes. Very soon after that, she must jump into a cab, and guess who her driver is? Of course it's the same cabdriver. Guess what he now has stocked in his cab? Eyedrops. It's a very simple but effective touch.

So setups and payoffs don't always have to have a

middle. But ones that are more important to the overall story usually should.

Johnny Gets a Call from Mommy

While training to become an astronaut, Johnny gets a call from his mommy, who contacts him via Internet videoconferencing. She's responding to a frightfully hateful letter Johnny left in her mailbox the night he stalked her family (which was the setup). She wants to clear the air. Mommy tells Johnny that the reason she left was that his psycho father threatened to kill her if she didn't.

This exchange represents the middle of a subplot. And it's interesting. Maybe Johnny doesn't believe his mommy. She could be a lying lunatic. How is he to know? Gives his character a dilemma.

The story progresses; Johnny and Daddy are locked in hand-to-hand combat. It's near the story's climax, and Daddy is about to kill Johnny. Suddenly, a picture of Mommy falls out of Daddy's pocket.

Yes, Daddy admits, he *does* still love Mommy after all these years. And yes, Daddy admits, he forced Mommy to leave.

Johnny is pissed. He opens up a can of whup-ass and kills Daddy.

Mommy's picture represents the third and final time we see her in the movie (the payoff).

Mommy's small but important role in the story had a beginning, middle, and end: a setup, middle, and payoff.

A What?

Johnny's mommy and the way she appears and reappears in the story represent what is called a motif. A motif is a recurrence of an important element in your story. This element could be a character, an image, and/or a piece of dialogue.

Motifs in stories seem to work best if you repeat these important story elements three times. It doesn't *always* have to be three times. And you don't have to do this with *all* things in your story. Don't go crazy. Just consider that there are certain things in your story that you may include one (beginning), two (middle), and three (end) times.

These motifs or repetitions help you achieve economy of story by recycling important story elements.

Motifs are important in your script to help you build a theme for your movie—but we're not even going to get into *that*.

Avoid the Storytelling Traps

Beyond thinking of your story and its important elements in terms of beginning, middle, and end, remember that your story is a journey. And during the journey, exciting things must happen.

If you are still having a hard time coming up with exciting things to happen in your story, perhaps you aren't working with the right concept yet. I don't want you to think that by exciting I mean car chases or gun battles or anything. Small moments in movies where two characters simply talk to each other can be very exciting. These moments may be exciting because they're dramatic, funny, or realistic. At the very least, they are interesting.

For your story to work, you should strive for a story that is logical but creative. Grounded in reality, but totally unique. Your scenes have to build logically onto each other, like LEGO bricks. This one goes here, this one goes there. It all fits.

Avoid putting stuff in your script for no good reason. If you have scenes like that in your story, you're probably working with a contrivance.

Avoid contrivances like cold sores.

"Contrivance," "Cliché," "Insipid"— Dirty Words You Need to Learn

A contrivance is something you put in your story to make the story work. Contrivances usually seem forced— that is, they don't really fit into the script naturally. It could be a character who doesn't really belong or something that happens in a scene that doesn't really fit or that seems to come out of nowhere. Contrivances stop a story from flowing.

You will probably use a contrivance in your script when you try to make your story work. You are *forcing* your story to work. Unfortunately, it never does.

Besides contrivances, you should avoid other pitfalls.

"Cliché" is a word the people in Hollywood who are paid to review scripts (remember, the Big Fancy Hollywood Readers?) can't live without. Their use of the word "cliché" is in itself a cliché, but it's their favorite word. A cliché in scripts generally refers to a story element or character that has been done a thousand times already, something that's unoriginal, hackneyed, overused.

"Banal" is another word readers with a thesaurus will use when they've used "cliché" too much. And don't forget "trite"!

"Insipid" is a word you don't want a reader to use to describe your script. It means the Big Fancy Hollywood Reader thought your story was dull. I've already discussed the dangers of being dull.

To avoid having a Big Fancy Hollywood Reader write any of those words about your script (and they will write this about your script when they do what is called coverage), you need to be original with your storytelling and find a way to write a fresh script.

If you want to write the best script you possibly can write, try to write an organic story.

The Perfect Organism

An organic story is one that unfolds naturally and seems effortless and flowing.

It's difficult to write an organic story; it might take you many years to perfect that way of storytelling. Just try to recognize contrivances and avoid the impulse to force your story to be a certain way. Avoid clichés. Make your story as naturally exciting as possible.

If you let it develop naturally, your story may go in a direction you haven't considered. This might be frustrating because it means you are never really on top of your story and you may have to replot. But your creativity, which is smarter than you are (because it sees the beauty of your story before you are consciously aware of it), knows what it's doing and will do it correctly if you let it.

Okay, enough Zen. Just try to write as natural a script as possible.

More Words About Big Fancy Hollywood Readers

Earlier I brought up the Big Fancy Hollywood Readers, and if you haven't noticed from my tone, I dislike them.

Unfortunately, they are a very important part of Hollywood. Why? Well, usually the first person to read your script in Hollywood is a Big Fancy Hollywood Reader. (They are actually called readers, but I like to call them Big Fancy Hollywood Readers because that's what they think they are.)

Therefore, as much as I hate to say this, in many ways you should try to write a script that will appeal to the Big Fancy Hollywood Readers. So I want to tell you about a thing many of the Big Fancy Hollywood Readers will claim your story needs for it to be successful. That concept is called the ticking clock.

Two Days Before You Die!

A ticking clock is a plot device that gives a story urgency.

Here's a good analogy. Say your bladder is full and you have to pee. Someone is in the bathroom and won't come out.

You've got yourself a ticking clock.

A ticking clock means that a character or characters in your movie have to do something in an allotted amount of time or something (usually bad) will happen to them or someone they love.

I have read things Big Fancy Hollywood Readers have written about scripts they don't like, and they go a little something like this: "The story was clichéd, the writing lacked freshness, and the script really could have used a ticking clock."

For some reason, Big Fancy Hollywood Readers are obsessed with ticking clocks. They think any story without one is a bad story.

My view on ticking clocks is that they are overrated. If you write a movie solely around a ticking clock concept, you might write a contrived and trite script.

However, ticking clocks do offer your story a potentially exciting hook. A story propelled by a ticking clock is more urgent. A story with urgency tends to be more interesting.

If a ticking clock fits organically into your story, then add the ticking clock. If there's no room for one, then don't add one. Just be aware that Big Fancy Hollywood Readers really, really like them.

The movie *Speed* uses a variation of the ticking clock concept in an interesting way. Rather than facing a ticking clock, the lead character in the movie faces a ticking bomb that will explode if a bus carrying passengers goes below fifty miles per hour. It's a clever variation of the ticking clock concept.

K.I.S.S. but Keep Us Guessing

When you develop your story, you will be walking a tightrope.

On one hand, if your story is predictable and has been done a thousand times already, what will the audience find interesting? If your story is too predictable, you probably won't ever sell your script.

On the other hand, you won't engage an audience if you develop a story that's too complicated.

The surest way to keep an audience interested is to keep them wondering what's going to happen next. So as you work and rework your story outline, you have a lot to think about. Your goal is to create a story that is logical and economical, recycles important story elements, and is above all other things interesting.

What you really want is a good, tight story. A good, tight story is like a snake in a figure eight eating its tail. A good story always comes *back* to itself and is complete.

CHAPTER 4

Characters, Conflict, Relationships, Oh My!

Your story will probably have a lead character. That's your protagonist. A bunch of other supporting characters will also be in your movie. Something obviously must happen to your characters. They are kicked around, learn some lessons, and, by the end of the story, become older and wiser. And just as your story should be interesting, the characters in your movie must be interesting.

What makes a character interesting? When he or she has something to overcome, learn, or fight against?

Let's not put the cart before the horse.

The best characters are the ones who seem like real human beings. Real people do things and speak words.

So your characters will take action and speak dialogue.

Let's talk first about the action your characters take.

Your Characters' Actions

In your movie, your characters will take action for two reasons: something happens that causes them to do something (they are reacting), or they decide to do something in order to obtain what they want (they take action to achieve a goal). In both cases, your characters' actions are the results of decisions they make.

Well, your characters aren't making the decisions. *YOU* are.

As your characters develop, however, a funny thing happens. Characters *will* start making their own choices. It's a strange concept, but when you write a scene and let the character take over, you'll know what I mean.

In reality, though, *you* are the puppet master. The audience must never see you pulling the strings. The most obvious way the audience will feel a character isn't real is when your characters say, or more importantly, *do* illogical things.

Here, Kitty, Kitty

Here's an example of an illogical character choice:

Danica, a character in a horror story, is home one night watching the evening news, and it's reported that a psycho killer is on the loose. She hears a noise outside. She grabs a flashlight and walks into the woods to investigate.

The audience is throwing popcorn at this point. "Deserves to die, deserves to die," they chant. Why would a sane person go outside with a killer on the loose? Danica made a really illogical decision.

Let's make it a little more logical. Danica watches the news, hears a noise outside. She is worried about her cat and can't find it anywhere. She is afraid she might have locked the fleabag outside. Despite news of a killer on the loose, Danica goes outside.

Nope.

The audience still won't buy it. A cat? I wouldn't risk my life for my cats (sorry, C.G.). I know some people would, but most sane people wouldn't.

Characters Aren't Stupid, Your Story Is!

Most of the time a character in your movie will make an illogical choice because you've already plotted out your story. You wrote in your story outline (and later in your treatment) that Danica goes outside and is killed.

You can't just think of Danica as a character who does whatever your story calls for. You have to think of her as a *real* human being, even if she only has a small role in your story.

If your characters do not behave like real humans, it is quite possible you have not figured out why they take the actions they take or why they make their decisions. You are simply plugging them into your story.

Characters are not drain stoppers. You, the writer, must know why your character takes an action or makes a decision.

Dumb and Dumber

Your story has a problem if your character makes illogical choices.

That is not to say your characters cannot make *stupid* choices. Real people make real decisions. For your characters to seem real, they might make stupid choices.

Drinking while driving is never smart, and yet a character might do it.

A girl stays in an abusive relationship. While stupid, this is often the case.

A guy continues to do drugs even though they're ruining his life. Stupid, but this too is commonplace.

Remember that you're striving to create real people. Real people do stupid things, or stay stuck in stupid situations, because they don't have the smarts to do otherwise, even if they are intelligent people. So characters may say or do stupid things in your story. But characters should not do illogical things.

Strengthen the Motivation

Fixing your characters' illogical decisions or actions is easy. Give them a stronger motivation to make a decision or take an action.

Why not have Danica venture outside to save her sister? Or her boyfriend? You could even have her face a ticking clock. Explosives are rigged to her house, and if she doesn't brave the woods and the killer, she faces certain doom.

If your character makes a decision and takes an action, the audience must believe this character has good motivation. Your character can't go outside and run into the knife of a killer simply because you wrote in your story outline, "Danica goes outside and is killed."

Again, you need to think of Danica as a real person who makes real decisions based on her motivation. Give her real motivation, not something stupid. (Okay, a cat *could* work. But not my cat.)

Motivation causes characters to make a real decision. Motivation propels the characters forward in their story. So give your characters stronger motivations to make their decisions. That in turn will make your characters stronger.

Make Your Characters Important

I wrote a romantic comedy called *I.C.Q. (I Seek You)* that features a protagonist, Melanie Harris, who falls in love with Victor Steele, a movie star. Melanie must hide the fact that she wants to be an actress because Victor is famous and sensitive about people's motives for befriending him: do they love the real him or the illusion?

In the script, Melanie has a confidante, Christine, her best friend, who provides comic relief and also supports Melanie in her pursuit of Victor. In early drafts of the script, Christine came off as a caricature. She was big, brassy, and not very graceful. She was also slightly pathetic because she seemed like the type of person who lived her life through someone else—in this case, Melanie.

Christine didn't really have a strong reason to be in the script other than that I needed a best friend for Melanie. There was no other point to her existence.

I loved Christine. She was funny and good-hearted, but I needed to find a stronger reason for her to be in the script. The solution was simple: rather than make Christine simply a best friend, I gave her an active role in Melanie's story.

Remember how Melanie wants to be an actress? Christine became Melanie's best friend *and* agent.

An example of economy by accomplishing two things at once with the character.

If Melanie succeeds in her quest to get Victor Steele, then nothing but good things will happen for Christine's business . . . or so she thinks. In later drafts of the scripts, greed and self-interest became part of Christine's motivation, and they added a whole dimension to her personality that hadn't existed before. Her motivation made her more real. Christine's being Melanie's agent really opened up parts of the story I hadn't considered.

Motivation for your characters is not very difficult to figure out. It's an extremely important element for all the characters in your movie, though. A properly motivated character makes decisions the way real people do.

So properly motivate your characters, and it will take you a long way toward creating believable characters. The audience will greatly appreciate that.

Give Your Characters Goals

Besides motivation, there is another thing your characters will probably need that is particularly important to Big Fancy Hollywood Readers.

Your characters—particularly your protagonist—most likely should have a goal.

Everybody wants something, right? You want the million bucks! Your protagonist and other characters in your movie should *want* something. The reason your characters should have goals is simple: the audience will *care* about your character. If your character reaches their goal, the audience might erupt into cheers. If your character does not reach their goal, the audience might cry.

Audiences like to cheer and they like to cry. If your character reaches or fails to reach a goal, this gives the audience an investment in your character.

Big Fancy Hollywood Readers are adamant that your characters—particularly your protagonist—must have goals. I absolutely agree with the readers that it is important for your character to want something. Like I said, *everybody* wants something. That's human. My problem with this whole business of goals is this: Big Fancy Hollywood Readers want to see a character who absolutely *must* achieve something (their goal) or the world will fall apart! It's a life-or-death goal! But goals may be subtler than that.

Waylon and the Million-Dollar Disaster

Here is an example of the problem you might face trying to develop a concept based on a character with one big goal.

Let's say a friend tells you about a character concept. Waylon is a computer hack who wants to be a millionaire before he is eighteen.

And you're like, "Okay, so what happens?"

Your friend says that's the concept.

As a good friend, you should say that Waylon needs a motivation for wanting a million dollars. Waylon's smaller, more human goals need to be developed.

Perhaps you could suggest that Waylon doesn't just want a million bucks. Waylon wants to prove to a fellow computer hacker that his hacking abilities are superior. Also, he wants to steal the million bucks from a bank that turned him down for a scholarship. Waylon is now motivated by arrogance and revenge. These are smaller goals. The million bucks is the big goal.

Let's say Waylon hacks into the bank and fulfills his goal of being a millionaire before he turns eighteen.

If he even *makes* it to eighteen.

The account he hacked into belongs to an international terrorist organization. And they do not think too kindly of the theft.

Waylon's goal to be a millionaire has developed into a potentially interesting concept for a movie. His goal has become multitiered. He wants money (most important goal). But he also wants to prove to a competitor that he can get it (a smaller goal). He wants to take revenge on the bank that dissed him (a smaller goal). Waylon now has the potential to be an interesting character.

Goals Come Big and Small

The problem you face by giving a character just one big goal is that the character may come off as one-dimensional. One-dimensional characters are artificial and lame. You want three-dimensional characters who are fully developed and seem real.

Getting back to *I.C.Q. (I Seek You)*, Melanie's main goal is to win the affection of Victor Steele. Yet if that was her only goal—to snag some guy—Melanie would be one-dimensional. She would be shallow and her story wouldn't be very interesting.

Melanie's goal is Victor Steele, yes. But Melanie doesn't *only* want Victor. She also wants independence from her overbearing father. On top of which, she wants a shot at something she truly loves: acting.

Melanie has one big goal (Victor) and several small ones (independence from her father and a career as an actress).

Christine, her agent, also has goals. Christine wants her best friend to be happy and to find the man of her dreams. Christine *also* wants Melanie to snag Victor because it will help her agent business.

So characters need goals. Don't just give them one big goal. Give them subtler goals too. That's a way of ensuring that your characters are believable and three-dimensional.

Mother of All Conflicts

Another way to ensure that your story and characters are interesting is to create complications or conflicts for your characters. Complications are synonymous with conflicts, by the way. For clarity's sake, I will use the word "conflict."

A conflict is something that stands in the way of what your character wants. A person, thing, or event could provide a conflict. The conflict challenges your character and makes it difficult for them to achieve their goal. It creates tension, which is a good thing. It makes the audience more interested in your story.

Characters become more interesting when a conflict arises and they must overcome it.

Innies and Outies—The Difference Between Internal and External Conflict

Conflicts do not always happen *to* a character. Conflicts may come from *within* a character. (You've heard the term "drama queen," right?)

Internal conflicts are tricky to pull off, but they can be powerful. An internal conflict is something a character feels or believes that causes an external problem or conflict.

Perhaps you have a character who has known since he was little that he would marry a girl from the Jewish faith. The guy falls in love with a girl who is not Jewish. This presents an internal conflict. His belief system is challenged.

Internal conflicts often lead to external conflicts.

Let's say this guy's mother insists that he stop seeing the girl. *That* is an external conflict.

Then the guy debates in his head—Who do I listen to, my mom or my heart? That's internal.

What if he decides that his conflict has never been within him? He realizes he only wanted to marry a girl of the Jewish faith because his *mother* wanted him to.

This represents a dynamic explosion between internal and external conflict.

Guilt is an internal conflict. Rage starts internally. Revenge starts internally. Shyness is internal.

Internal conflicts usually manifest themselves in some external way.

The point is to get you to think of your characters as living, breathing people who are not all about their actions. They also think and feel.

Internal conflicts are tricky but can be very effective.

The Motif of the Suicidal Father

In the movie *The Game*, the lead character must face a conflict caused by his father's suicide (he jumped off a building when the protagonist was young). The suicide is expressed through a motif, though in this case the motif is shown through grainy home movies and family photos that appear six (not three) times throughout the movie.

The motif gives insight into the character's motivation. Much of what happens to the character is caused by the father's suicide. The protagonist tries throughout the movie to overcome the power his father's death has over him. This is an internal conflict, and it propels the entire movie.

And while *The Game*'s resolution is hokey, the motif of the suicidal father represents an interesting case study in the power of an internal conflict in shaping a story.

I'm Gonna Kick Your . . .

External conflicts are used much more often in films, and they are very powerful. Most external conflicts are caused by a disagreement between the protagonist and the antagonist.

When someone or something stands in the way of what a character wants, *that* is the antagonist. The antagonist adds conflict to the protagonist's life. Or, if there is no goal involved, the antagonist simply makes life very difficult for the protagonist.

Your protagonist usually needs at least one antagonist. Maybe there are several.

The type of movie you write will determine what kind of antagonist you will need.

Some movies do not seem to have an antagonist at all.

If you look closely enough, though, you will find something that stands in the way of your lead character's goals.

As I mentioned before, the antagonist might not be a person but a thing. The shark in *Jaws* was the main antagonist. The antagonist can also be weather, such as a tornado. In scary movies, the antagonist could be an alien or monster that goes around killing everyone. An antagonist can also be something somewhat benign, like a kid sister who is always foiling your lead character's plans.

Remember, your script may have more than one antagonist. But don't forget about economy and recycling. The fewer story elements (e.g., antagonists) you work with, the tighter your script.

In my script *I.C.Q. (I Seek You),* Melanie's father stands in the way of her goal of independence and winning the heart of Victor Steele. He actively works *against* her goals. That makes him an antagonist. Even though he's a decent guy, he's Melanie's antagonist.

Melanie also has an even stronger antagonist in the form of Victor Steele's mother. She's the *real* adversary (another way of saying antagonist).

The Golden Arches

Another important factor in creating interesting characters is giving them an arc. An arc is a fancy way of saying that your characters change, grow, and learn some lessons. They start out one way at the beginning of your movie, and by the end, they have changed in some big or perhaps even subtle but powerful way.

An arc means your character embarks on a quest and is transformed by his or her journey.

Remember Johnny, the young astronaut? A good way to give Johnny an arc is to ensure that when the story is over, he has changed drastically.

We know Johnny's goal is to become the youngest astronaut in space. And we know that by the end of the story, he will become an astronaut. So you don't want to start the story off with Johnny as an assistant astronaut. Make him the furthest thing from an astronaut. Like a fast-food worker.

Johnny's brilliant, yes, and talented. But he flips burgers.

That's an arc. Going from a fast-food worker to an astronaut!

Not that you have to be that extreme. Just remember, by giving your character an arc, you start them off in one place and by the end of the movie they have changed in some way. Even if it means they have gotten older, wiser, and a little bit more mature.

Recap of Writing Characters

Characters in your movie, especially the protagonist, should be properly motivated to take action. They should avoid illogical decisions. They should want something (their goal), but things should stand in the way of achieving that goal (conflicts).

1) Make sure your characters (particularly your protagonist) have good motivation for their choices.
2) Ensure that your characters' choices are logical (even if they are *stupid*).
3) Know *why* your characters make their choices.
4) See to it that your characters (particularly your protagonist) have a big investment in the outcome of the story (that is, they want something and have goals).
5) Give your characters an arc.

Where's My Posse?

Let's talk about the supporting players in your movie.

The most popular supporting player in a movie is the sidekick. A sidekick is usually the person closest to the protagonist who gives them advice, laughs at all their jokes, and makes them laugh or consoles them when they cry. The most popular sidekick is the best friend. The sidekick is usually the person in the story the protagonist turns to most when they are in need. There is usually one main sidekick, if there's a sidekick at all (there doesn't have to be).

Other very important supporting players in a movie are the "love interest," which should be pretty self-explanatory, and the "authority figure," who guides the protagonist through conflicts. The same rule for creating the protagonist is true for the sidekick and all supporting characters in your movie. Just make sure the character comes off real. The more real, the better.

And don't forget interesting.

Whack 'Em

When you start writing your story, you might find that you have a gazillion characters. There's the protagonist, an antagonist (or two), the sidekick, and then all these other characters who come in and out of the movie, never to be seen again.

Remember economy? Telling stories as economically as possible?

Economy applies to characters as well. If you can limit the number of characters in your movie by combining several characters into one, your story might be more focused. If the protagonist has two best friends, is there any way you can combine those characters?

There's nothing wrong with having a lot of characters, and if your story calls for them, definitely keep them in. *American Pie* features one protagonist who has several friends. The goal of the friends is to have sex. Each friend's unique story about his quest to have sex is important to the movie. It wouldn't work as well if all the friends were rolled into one character.

But the protagonist in *American Pie* had a clueless and dorky father who always came into his room at the worst conceivable time. What if the writer of the script had focused on the mother too? That would have been too much. The story would not have been as focused or as funny.

The point is, you should examine your story and see if you have any redundancies in characters. Does every character in your story have a purpose? Would your story lose value if you took out a particular character? Could you roll a couple of characters into one and still get what you need?

It's worth thinking about.

Develop Real Relationships

I personally have a difficult time understanding human relationships. As a writer, I spend so much time in my head that when I actually have to deal with other human beings, they confuse me.

This has been a problem in my earlier scripts. Because I was so focused on making a scene do what I wanted it to do, I forced my characters to interact in a way that came across as stilted. Their relationships didn't feel real or natural.

For characters to be good, they can't just be similar to real people. They must also have real *relationships* with the other people in your movie. Developing real relationships between characters will in turn create "emotional resonance" for your story.

As you develop characters and their relationships, plot

points might be torpedoed. That's totally okay. As your characters evolve and their relationships grow, your story may change. It happens. It's better, though, to reshape your story to fit an evolving character than it is to ram a character into a story just to make it work. Audiences won't tolerate characters who aren't believable.

Developing real relationships between your characters is an important part of creating believable characters and something to consider as you embark on writing your treatment.

CHAPTER 5

Are You Ready for Treatment?

Well, my friends, as I've said before, writing a screenplay is a journey. Along this journey so far, we have covered a lot of material. You're not expected to learn it all at once. It takes time to digest the material and make sense of it. Besides, writing is instinctive. You just do it.

So let's just do it and start working on your treatment. Before you gasp in horror and drop this book in fear, relax and remember—take as long as you need to accomplish the task of finding your story. Only when you find your story through the story outline will you start your treatment.

Spend as much time as you need working with your story outline before proceeding to treatment. Remember, your goal with the story outline is to figure out most of the scenes that will be in your movie.

It takes time to make the choices that help you discover your story. You might have a difficult time coming up with the scenes for your movie. That's okay. Sometimes you will find stories easily; other times it takes a while for the story to gel.

Perhaps you find that your story constantly changes. That's okay too. It most likely means your story is improving. You will toss, rearrange, and rewrite many of your story elements until you find the story that is right for you.

Hang in there.

Review previous chapters until you have a good story outline. Once you feel comfortable that you have found your story, it's is time to move to your treatment.

A treatment is an outline for most or all the scenes that will take place in your movie. Your treatment is based on your story outline. But where the story outline is general, the treatment is specific. Each scene that takes place in a script is conveyed in your treatment.

The way you choose to write your treatment is really up to you. There's no right or wrong way. Essentially, it's like writing a short story, but instead of being written in past tense, it's written in present tense. You may write a sentence or two describing each scene, or you may write a whole page. The more detail you provide for each scene, though, the easier it will be when it comes time to write your script. Writing a more detailed treatment will also help you spot potential story problems.

And as you begin writing your treatment, here's a really good tip to help bring your scenes to life.

Visualize Your Scenes

Movies are mostly visual. Sure, sound is important.

But movies are not radio. Movies are images. That means what the audience sees on the screen is very important.

When you start writing your treatment, it's a very good idea to spend some time visualizing a scene in your head before you write about it. Close your eyes and put on music that inspires you. Zone out. Picture each scene in your head. Pretend you are watching your scene on the movie screen. *Really* try to imagine the scene.

What's happening?

Write things down. Whatever comes to you.

The treatment mainly focuses on the action in your movie, though writing dialogue is certainly okay. Visualize the scene and then write about it. What do you see? Where does the scene take place? How does the scene begin? What happens? How does the scene end? What action do your characters take in the scene?

By the time you are done with this exercise, you should have a treatment that explains the details of each scene that will be in your movie.

Once you get through all the scenes, spend some time reworking your treatment. Add details, cut unnecessary things. Reread this section, then go back over your treatment and reevaluate your story and characters. Change things. Improve them. Make the story tighter. Make your characters more real.

When you're finished writing your treatment, you will have a solid blueprint of your story.

Well done!

SECTION THREE

How Cute–
Your First Script

CHAPTER 1

Look, Ma, I'm Doing It!
(And It's Not What You Think)

Hopefully by this point you have worked on your treatment and quite possibly it is finished.

If you're having trouble completing your treatment, then most likely you're having difficulty coming up with a story outline. If you're having difficulty with a story outline, most likely you're not working with the right concept.

If that's the case, then perhaps you need to start fresh, with a new concept.

Or you need to consider working with a partner.

Working with a Partner

I am a very independent person. When I first started writing, I wanted to write what I wanted when I wanted.

I made very little progress in terms of selling my work.

Don't get me wrong; I developed immensely as a writer. I spent a few years writing script after script, doing them exactly the way I wanted. But for the first few years, I didn't get very far in Hollywood.

Probably the most wonderful thing I did for myself as a writer was to work with a partner.

If you happened to read the dedication in this book, you will see that it is to Shannon, who was my first writing partner. Shannon and I met when I was nineteen years old (the age I started writing) and became close. A few years later Shannon and I thought—Hey, why not write a script together?

One night we sat around and hashed out a story. Then we did the story outline, and once we had a good handle on the story, we wrote a ten-page treatment. We really didn't know what we were doing, so we started shopping our story to Hollywood before we even had a script. We landed a meeting at MGM. The executive who met with us wasn't very friendly. I'm not sure why she even came to the meeting. She assumed we were pitching a full-length script and we were like, "Um, well, we only have a treatment!"

She irritably asked us to tell her the story. We blurted it out. Midway into the meeting the woman became someone very different. She was getting our story. She liked it. By the end, she loved our story *and* us. She said, "Go home and write this script and don't tell anyone else about the story." She didn't want us to be ripped off.

We were stoked. We divvied up the scenes. Shannon wrote some, I wrote the others. Then, once we'd assembled the scenes, we had the first draft of our script. A few drafts later, we landed an agent. He was at a small agency but had some influence. After a few months with that agent, we landed an agent at a bigger agency.

The moral of this story is twofold. One, write your treatment. Two, consider working with a partner.

It's half the money but twice the fun!

Finalizing Your Treatment

Whether you work solo or with a partner, before you begin writing your script, make sure your treatment is ready.

Much like developing your concept, the best way to finalize your treatment is to evaluate the story:

1) Have you written up most or all of the scenes that will be in your movie?
2) Have you completed the necessary research to ensure you can comfortably write about the people, places, or events in your script?
3) Are there any holes in your story?
4) Did you stick to a genre?
5) Did you tell your story economically?
6) Is every scene necessary?
7) Are there any characters who can be combined?
8) Do all the setups in your story pay off?
9) Could you use a motif?
10) Does your story have any contrivances or clichés?
11) Could you add a ticking clock for urgency?
12) Does each scene propel your story forward?

13) Will your story keep the audience guessing or is it too complicated?

14) Do you have enough conflicts/complications in your story?

15) Do your characters make logical decisions (even if they are bad decisions)?

16) Are your characters properly motivated?

17) Are the scenes organized in the proper fashion or could you reorder scenes to make them flow better?

Take some time with your treatment. Make sure it's the best it can be before you move on to writing a script.

Before you move on to the script, though, let's take a fresh look at the two most important ingredients of your movie: the descriptive passage and dialogue.

CHAPTER 2

Simple, Visual, Necessary—The Art of Thinking like a Moviemaker

When you begin a script, you will turn your treatment into scenes. These scenes will make up your script. Scenes (and thus your script) are mostly made up of two things: the descriptive passage and dialogue.

Earlier I mentioned that story is not any more important than character. The same is true with descriptive passages and dialogue.

So while it is no more important than dialogue, let's discuss the best way to approach the descriptive passage first.

Simple, Visual, and Necessary

A descriptive passage tells what will be *seen* on the movie screen. It provides descriptions of essential things in the scene and explains the action. Descriptive passages explain where a scene takes place and which characters are in the scene. If there are new characters, there might be a brief description of them. The descriptive passage also describes the action in the scene.

Remember, descriptive passages are *always* written in the present tense.

There are three simple but very important rules for writing kick-butt descriptive passages.

The very best descriptive passages are simple, visual, and necessary.

Simple

Simple descriptive passages are clean, easy to read, and easy to follow. The shorter the better. If you write long, wordy descriptive passages, you will be nailed for being a novice. Keep your descriptive passages simple. Nothing elaborate or confusing.

Get to the point.

And don't tell us what the character is thinking. You are not writing a novel. In descriptive passages, you tell us what your characters are *seeing* or *doing*.

Visual

Your descriptive passages should describe what will be seen on the movie screen. And what do you see on the movie screen? Images.

With descriptive passages, you are writing out the images that will be in your movie.

Some images may be boring. For instance, you might write, "She walks to the door." What will be seen on the movie screen is an actress who walks to a door.

Other images in the movie will be very exciting.

The Eruption

In *The Eruption,* a movie script about a volcano I cowrote with my partner, Shannon, we had to write out the final action sequence. A sequence is an arrangement of scenes that show an important event unfolding.

In the final sequence of *The Eruption,* the volcano erupts and destroys an entire town and the people in it. We couldn't just write, "The volcano erupts." Our job as the writers was to picture the scene and write it up in a visually interesting way. So here's what we wrote:

EXT. CITY STREETS — MORNING

It is chaotic, a mass of desperate CITIZENS eager to flee. A man pushes through the crowd, pointing to the volcano.

                    MAN
          The volcano is coming!
          The volcano is coming!

And indeed, she does.

EXT. VOLCANO — MORNING

Half a dozen tornados whip around the

volcano's summit. Smoke shoots into the air like a frantic gusher. Serpents of smoke pierce through the tornadoes and race to the city.

Fire shoots out of the volcano at an arc. Then black and red lava launches into the blue sky.
It's very colorful and surreal.

EXT. CITY STREETS — MORNING

Thick smoke blots the sun. Mass chaos as PEOPLE run and SCREAM. Suddenly, a supersonic BLAST sweeps people off the street, tossed like debris. The RUMBLING is ear shattering. Some pick themselves up. Dead people don't.

Fire rains everywhere.

The volcano spits out its cancer, a huge black cloud that launches toward the city.

The black cloud is a living thing, ever expanding, filled with fire and electricity. The ball of smoke is actually ash and fire, superheated beyond 5000 degrees.

Headed for 30,000 people...

PEOPLE see the cloud, know enough to run from it. The cloud chases them.

The black cloud snatches a running MAN and embraces him. The body is cooked to a charcoal husk. The husk topples over and shatters.

A WOMAN struggles against a wind shear of fire that turns her into a fireball. She is swept away and crashes into a house, swept off its support into another house. The whole concoction is an eruption of flames. Everything is turned to carbon skeletons, swept along with the force of hell.

A FAMILY huddled in a circle, PRAYING. Their home erupts into flames. They SCREAM, swept away by the roiling mass of fire.

You might have noticed that in the example from *The Eruption*, there were many different scenes and yet there were no sluglines. That's because it was a sequence of events. It's a stylistic choice to tell a sequence in one long scene. That way you don't disrupt the pacing of the sequence with sluglines.

Visualize Your Scene

To capture the scene visually and write out the descriptive passages, Shannon and I asked ourselves, "If we went to the movies, what would we want to see on the screen?" We sat down, closed our eyes, and imagined that sequence before we wrote it up.

Your job as the screenwriter is to come up with the nice visuals. Write your descriptive passages in a visually interesting way—this will add power to your script.

Necessary

Remember how we talked about economy when telling stories and writing characters? Well, the same is true with your descriptive passages. Necessary, in terms of writing your descriptive passages, means making sure there's a purpose for every word. Only put in details you *absolutely* need. Don't tell us what your character is wearing unless it's necessary. Don't tell us what your character is thinking. If you need to let us know he or she is nervous, tell us the character is fidgeting. Don't tell us the décor of a room in which a scene takes place unless it's necessary.

Make sure every word in your descriptive passage is necessary.

Economy of words really should be your mantra with descriptive passages (though not for dialogue, which I will explain later).

To recap: If your descriptive passage is simple, it will be easy to read. If it's visual, it will be interesting to read. If it's necessary, it will be important to read.

In the first draft, though, don't worry too much about writing perfect descriptive passages. Write as much as you need to get the scene out of you and on paper. You will tighten descriptive passages later in the rewrites. I just wanted to tell you about simple, visual, and necessary now so you at least begin to think of your descriptive passages in those ways.

CHAPTER 3

Like, Duh, Okay—You Know What I'm Talkin' 'Bout!

As you know, besides descriptive passages, the most important part of your movie will be dialogue. Dialogue represents the words that characters speak in your movie.

Dialogue in your script serves three important functions: it reveals a character's personality, it reveals relationships between characters, and it reveals story.

Writing dialogue is a paradox—it is at once simple and difficult. It is simple because your dialogue should be natural, and we hear natural dialogue every day.

Writing dialogue is difficult for two reasons:

First, not every person you meet speaks in the same manner. Therefore, not every character in your script will speak in the same manner. Some people speak very informally, with lots of "like's" and "um's" and hip phrases. Other characters speak in a more reserved fashion. Some characters don't speak much at all—they reveal themselves more through action than dialogue.

The second reason dialogue can be difficult is that you

will try to cram a lot of information about your story into your character's dialogue. This is called expository dialogue.

Exposition Isn't Just a Really Big Fair

Expository dialogue is when you explain important parts of your story through dialogue. Important information about your story could also be called exposition.

If you relay too much information about your story through dialogue, or if you don't relay it in the right way, some problems might appear. Dialogue loaded with too much exposition might sound wooden or artificial. Or the dialogue will be too "on the nose," which means the dialogue is obvious. Big Fancy Hollywood Readers will use that phrase a lot—the dialogue was too "on the nose."

The reason for wooden, artificial, or too on-the-nose dialogue, again, is that you're trying to cram too much important information into your characters' dialogue.

Exposition in dialogue usually comes out when you're trying to relay important backstory or story information.

```
              CHARACTER
        Oh, I have to go to the
        store now because my dad
        is abusive and if I
        don't get him his
        cigarettes right away he
        will become a monster.
```

This bit of dialogue is wrong on *many* levels.

The main reason dialogue like this doesn't work is simple: too much information is given. There's no subtlety. It's too obvious.

Beginning writers often load their dialogue up with too much exposition. They do this because they don't understand that important information in a scene can be revealed through action rather than dialogue.

Here's another example of too much exposition in dialogue:

Say you have a story where a girl, Alberta, is haunted by the death of her grandmother, who was her caretaker. The grandmother died a decade ago, but the death still haunts Alberta.

Alberta is now a runaway living on the streets of Hollywood. She is twenty and has been on her own since she was ten. Alberta meets a kid named Stuart who has a similar story; his sister died a few years back, and she was the one who raised him.

One night Alberta and Stuart tell each other their stories. They tell their stories through dialogue.

No.

You are *not* writing a play. You are writing a *movie.* Movies are mainly told through visual images. An audience does not want to hear Alberta and Stuart talk about their pasts for an entire movie. An audience wants to *see* what happened rather than be *told* what happened through dialogue.

Kindergarten with a Twist

There is a rule in most forms of writing, including screenwriting, that states you should *show* and not *tell*.

When people read your script, they don't want everything spelled out for them through dialogue. They would rather *see* what is happening in your story. So *show* scenes in your movie that explain your story instead of *telling* us what has already happened. In other words, show us your story through action rather than telling the story through a character's dialogue.

And if you do reveal important information through dialogue, try not to telegraph it. Try to make the information come out through the dialogue in a subtle way.

Just remember to ask yourself: is there a better way to reveal important story information than through dialogue? Can important information be revealed through action instead?

Dialogue Is Not Always Economical

We've discussed the importance of economy in terms of developing your story and writing your descriptive passages. Economy does *not* necessarily apply to dialogue.

When I first started writing scripts, I read many how-to screenwriting books that said I should try to write dialogue that was tight and sparse, meaning keep it short and sweet.

That's not good advice at all.

COLTON LAWRENCE (30s) sits in the
office of a BIG FANCY HOLLYWOOD READER
(20s).

                    COLTON
          Sure, my first script
          was a pitiful mess. It
          showed some naive
          talent, but the dialogue
          sucked. You know why?

                    READER
               (bored)
          Why?

                    COLTON
               (worked up)
          'Cause of those stupid
          books!

                    READER
          What books?

                    COLTON
          The books. The books!
          The screenwriting books
          that said to keep my
          dialogue short! So

that's what I did. But
you know what? People
like to talk! I
personally like to
ramble. Because I
followed the advice in
those books, though, my
characters talked in
clipped little machine-
gun bursts of info that
never sounded real. You
know why?

                    READER
          (frightened, backs
          away)
     Why?

                    COLTON
     Because in real life,
     people talk! A lot! Look
     at us, we're talking,
     huh?

Big Fancy Hollywood Reader rushes out
of the office. Keeps a wary eye on the
unpredictable, crazy writer.

Dialogue doesn't always have to be brisk and tight. Often a character has a lot to say. It might not be clean or perfect, but it should be real.

Go for real. Don't worry so much about economy.

While you should avoid monologues (that is, when a character talks forever and a day), let your characters talk. They might have something important and interesting to say!

It wasn't until I saw *Thelma and Louise* and then read the script that I realized it's okay (and even powerful) to let your characters talk! Don't be afraid to let your characters say what's on their minds.

Just follow the rules of three.

The Three Rules of Good Dialogue

Three good rules to follow with dialogue are:

1) Make sure characters don't all sound the same.

Don't go crazy with this. If your story features three cheerleaders from a wealthy suburban high school, they will speak, to some degree, in the same way.

But remember: even though three cheerleaders from a wealthy suburban high school are similar, they aren't the same character. Their relationships are different. Their stories are different. Otherwise, they *would* be the same character.

2) Show, don't tell.

Before a character reveals something important about

the story through dialogue, consider whether you might reveal the information through action instead.

3) Make sure the dialogue sounds real.

Let your characters talk. But remember, you're also telling a story. The dialogue should be important to the story.

When you become comfortable with writing dialogue, you'll develop an ear for it. You'll learn when dialogue works and when it doesn't.

An Example of Dialogue

```
FADE IN:


EXT. NEW YORK BROWNSTONE BUILDING —
NIGHT


Looking in windows of a brownstone
building to reveal conflict, conflict,
and conflict. Between people of all
races, ages, sexes:


WOMAN argues with a MAN. Two MEN argue.
Two ELDERLY PEOPLE argue.


Dogs BARK and babies CRY.


It's an unsettling pastiche of friction.
```

Look inside one window and it appears one couple isn't arguing. In fact, a romantic candlelit dinner is underway.

INT. CASSANDRA FOLEY'S DINING ROOM — NIGHT

Upon closer inspection, CASSANDRA FOLEY (20s) and TREY RUSSELL (20s) eat their candlelit dinner in seething silence.

> CASSANDRA (V.O.)
> That's Trey. He's a model. Gor-ge-*us*. One of his many problems is that he knows it. But he's stupid. New York is actually a very small city and I have friends everywhere. He thought he could get away with seeing that waif creature that passes herself off as a model without me finding out? He was *sadly* mistaken.

Cassandra looks up from her dinner and watches Trey eat. He senses her looking at him but doesn't look her in the eyes.

CASSANDRA (V.O.)
Before I did something
terrible, I wanted him
to have a chance to come
clean and express his
undying devotion to me.
After all, to be
worshiped as a goddess,
is that *bad*?

Trey finally looks up, finished with his dinner. Cassandra, who barely ate a thing, wipes her mouth.

CASSANDRA (V.O.)
Anyway, let's see what
Trey has to say for
himself.

TREY
Are you on the rag?

CASSANDRA

Excuse me?

TREY

You always get
premenstrually paranoid
when it's that
unfortunate time.

CASSANDRA

How would you know
anything about my
period? We've only known
each other two weeks.

TREY

Well, if you're like
most girls, you're
premenstrually paranoid,
is all I'm saying.

CASSANDRA

Guilty much?

TREY

What do I have to be

guilty about? I mean ...
we just met. So what if I
was with someone else?

                CASSANDRA
You admit it, then?

                TREY
I'm talking
hypotheticals here. So
what if I was with
another girl? I don't
owe you anything.

                CASSANDRA
Oh, I see. "You're the
most special girl in the
world," or "I can really
see us being together a
long time," or, my
favorite, "I know this
is crazy, it's only been
a few days, but I think
I love you."
        (beat)
What were those? *Hmmmm?*
I'm waiting.

                    TREY
Don't be naive.

                  CASSANDRA
Don't call me naive.
Don't *ever* call me
naive!

                    TREY
Let's just drop the
interrogation already.

                  CASSANDRA
You know, Trey, I *think*
I'm gonna have a problem
with that. I'm the kind
of girl who takes girly-
boys at their word. And
when they don't stick to
their word, that makes
me angry. And I don't
want some poor girl
falling for a cheap
little line and end up
pregnant or devastated
because she believed a
liar.

                    TREY
        Is this a revenge dinner?

                  CASSANDRA
        Now you're catching on.

This is a scene from my story *We Bitched!,* about a
young witch who turns her ex-boyfriends into female
dogs. It's loaded with exposition, but I think in the context of the story the exposition works.

Let's go through it piece by piece.

                CASSANDRA (V.O.)
            That's Trey. He's a
            model. Gor-ge-*us*. One of
            his many problems is
            that he knows it. But
            he's stupid. New York is
            actually a very small
            city and I have friends
            everywhere. He thought
            he could get away with
            seeing that waif
            creature that passes
            herself off as a model
            without me finding out?
            He was *sadly* mistaken.

First off, as you may remember, a character's name when they speak dialogue is always capitalized. Always, always, always.

Next to CASSANDRA, there is the parenthetical (V.O.). Remember, this means voice-over. You use voice-over when the voice of a character is heard over a particular scene, but they are not *in* the scene. The voice-over provides narration. Use (V.O.) sparingly, generally when you are explaining backstory. Many Big Fancy Hollywood Readers will say that if you use (V.O.) too much, you are *telling* too much of the story, rather than *showing* it.

In the dialogue example, this is what is being told: Cassandra's boyfriend, Trey, is a model, and he has been seeing another model behind her back. He doesn't know Cassandra knows.

I chose to begin with (V.O.) so I could develop Cassandra's voice—her particular way of speaking. I can tell you, though, that a Big Fancy Hollywood Reader would be skeptical reading a script that started out this way. Normally, a script that begins with a character speaking in (V.O.) spells trouble.

I could have substituted the (V.O.) and instead shown Cassandra at a bar watching Trey flirt with another girl. Instead, I chose to start my movie off as they were having dinner. I wanted Cassandra's voice to be heard. It's a choice I made. Hopefully the dialogue is strong enough that it works. It has taken me a long time to get to a place where expository dialogue works, though.

> CASSANDRA (V.O.)
> Before I did something
> terrible, I wanted him
> to have a chance to come
> clean and express his
> undying devotion to me.
> After all, to be
> worshiped as a goddess,
> is that *bad*?

I love this exposition because it says many things about Cassandra's character: she has an edge, she has a forgiving heart, and she is romantic, shallow, and perhaps insecure. Good dialogue reveals a lot about a character's personality.

> TREY
> Are you on the rag?

Trey reveals he's an immature dolt.

> TREY
> You always get
> premenstrually paranoid
> when it's that
> unfortunate time.

                    CASSANDRA

How would you know
anything about my
period? We've only known
each other two weeks.

                       TREY

Well, if you're like
most girls, you're
premenstrually paranoid,
is all I'm saying.

                    CASSANDRA

Guilty much?

                       TREY

I'm talking hypotheticals
here. So what if I was
with another girl?   I
don't owe you anything.

   The dialogue accomplishes a couple of things. First, it
establishes that they've only known each other for a few
weeks. It's a bit absurd for Cassandra to feel slighted that
Trey was with someone else. She's also immature, perhaps?
   Also, the dialogue between the two has a sense of banter. Banter is usually playful dialogue that's brisk and
swift. It's interplay between the characters, and it's fun to

watch. The dialogue from *We Bitched!* might have a serious tone, but in light of the fact that they've only known each other for two weeks, it's really just silly.

> CASSANDRA
> Oh, I see. "You're the
> most special girl in the
> world," or "I can really
> see us being together a
> long time," or, my
> favorite, "I know this
> is crazy, it's only been
> a few days, but I think
> I love you."
> (beat)
> What were those? *Hmmmm?*
> I'm waiting.

More exposition. Obviously, Trey is a player and likes to tell a girl what he thinks she wants to hear. Cassandra is calling him on it.

You will notice that in between Cassandra's dialogue is the word (beat). This is an action parenthetical. When a character speaks, you may want to break up the dialogue with some sort of action. In this case, the action is technically a pause. "Beat" in this case means a pause in dialogue or action.

Why not just write "pause"? It's another stupid thing

we screenwriters do. No one will shoot you, though, if you write "pause" instead of "beat".

You could instead substitute (beat) with (walks to the window) or some other action. Here's an example:

>   CASSANDRA
>   Oh, I see. "You're the
>   most special girl in the
>   world" or "I can really
>   see us being together a
>   long time," or, my
>   favorite, "I know this
>   is crazy, it's only been
>   a few days, but I think
>   I love you."
>   (walks to window)
>   What were those? *Hmmmm?*
>   I'm waiting.

Only use an action parenthetical inside dialogue if the action can be described in a few words. There's no need to say (*she* walks to the window) because we know who's walking to the window. You wouldn't use an action parenthetical to tell us that (*Trey* walks to the window) when Cassandra is speaking. You only use an action parenthetical to describe action taken by the character who is speaking.

Another thing. If your character's action is too long to

fit between the dialogue, you should split the dialogue up with a descriptive passage. Say for instance the phone rings and interrupts Cassandra. Here's a bad example of how to handle that situation:

CASSANDRA

Oh, I see. "You're the most special girl in the world," or "I can really see us being together a long time," or, my favorite, "I know this is crazy, it's only been a few days, but I think I love you."

>   (phone rings and she
>   moves to answer it,
>   then decides against
>   it)

What were those? *Hmmmm?* I'm waiting.

Instead, you should write:

CASSANDRA

Oh, I see. "You're the most special girl in the world," or "I can really

> see us being together a
> long time," or, my
> favorite, "I know this
> is crazy, it's only been
> a few days, but I think
> I love you."

The phone RINGS. Cassandra moves to answer it, but decides against it.

>   CASSANDRA (CONT)
>   What were those? *Hmmmm?*
>   I'm waiting?

You will notice that after CASSANDRA, there was the parenthetical (CONT). That means Cassandra continues to speak, even though a descriptive passage broke up her dialogue.

Action parentheticals should be short. If you need to break up dialogue with lengthier action, make that action into a descriptive passage. Try not to break up a character's dialogue too much, though. Breaking up dialogue tends to stop the rhythm or flow.

Back to Cassandra and Trey:

>   TREY
>   Don't be naive.

CASSANDRA

Don't call me naive.
Don't *ever* call me
naive!

Trey, again, is a dolt.

Cassandra has issues with being called naive, and this
comes out later in the story. She knows she's shallow,
but she never wants a person to mistake her as unintel-
ligent.

TREY

Let's just drop the
interrogation already.

CASSANDRA

You know, Trey, I *think*
I'm gonna have a problem
with that. I'm the kind
of girl who takes girly-
boys at their word. And
when they don't stick to
their word, that makes
me angry. And I don't
want some poor girl
falling for a cheap
little line and end up
pregnant or devastated

because she believed a
liar.

Cassandra reveals to Trey that she's about to open up a can of whup-ass. In this dialogue, she explains her motivation: men, even girly-boys, can be pigs. That makes her angry.

TREY
Is this a revenge dinner?

CASSANDRA
Now you're catching on.

Trey realizes he is screwed.

I hope the example illustrates that a lot of information can be conveyed through dialogue.

Exposition, particularly for beginning writers, is best used in moderation. Instead of revealing exposition in dialogue, see if you can reveal the information through your characters' actions.

The goal for your dialogue is to create a unique voice for each of your characters. Voice, as you will remember, is your way of viewing the world and writing it about it in a unique and compelling manner. Your characters should sound like real human beings.

In dialogue, you might also need to reveal important story information. It's a tricky balance and one that might take some time to get used to.

Don't Explain Too Much About How a Character Feels

Occasionally in a character's dialogue you will add a parenthetical that explains how a character feels.

CASSANDRA
(angry)
Now you're catching on.

The parenthetical (angry) is pointless in the previous example and clutters the script. It should be obvious how a character is feeling from their dialogue. If the feeling is not clear, then perhaps you need to clarify the dialogue or the context in which it's spoken so it's obvious how the character is supposed to be feeling.

If a parenthetical like (angry) *is* necessary, and sometimes it is, keep it tight. Avoid adverbs that end with -ly: (angrily), (bitterly), (tearfully), etc.

Punch it up and write: (angry), (bitter), (sobs).

Speaking of sobbing, it's time to begin your script.

CHAPTER 4

No More Drama (or Excuses)

By now, your treatment should be tight.

It should be clean.

It should be done.

Now you write the script.

And you have some good guidelines that should help you write a script that might even lead you to a million dollars.

But do you *really* want to write a script?

I suspect there are people reading this book who've realized that writing screenplays is not for them. And that's okay. The information in this book may be helpful even if you choose to write a short story, a poem, or a song.

Good storytelling is good storytelling. It doesn't matter what your medium or your goal. But you cannot and will not write a screenplay unless you have a total passion for it.

I hope you have a passion for it.

For Some of You—Goodbye

To get your first script, well, you have to write it.

If you're having a difficult time getting started, then

maybe you aren't meant to be a screenwriter. Maybe you need to work in a different arena for storytelling.

This book, though, will continue to focus on writing a script that may get you closer to making a million dollars. That was my promise, and I will deliver.

If you plan to write something other than a screenplay and we are parting ways, I bid you adieu and wish you the best of success in your development as a creative being.

For those of you who continue reading . . . let's write a screenplay!

Start at the Beginning

Once you've turned your story outline into a treatment and are ready to embark on your first script, here's the best place to start:

Page one.

The best thing to write, no surprise, is . . . scene one.

- Write FADE IN:.
- Write a slugline.
- Write a descriptive passage (or passages) and dialogue.

My friend, it is seriously that easy to write your first scene.

Most of your script will be made up of sluglines, descriptive passages, and dialogue. You get from the beginning to the end of your movie mostly with those three things. You write your movie one scene at a time.

Rather than think about writing your first scene, stop

thinking and just start writing. Overthinking the act of writing will be your biggest enemy.

Don't think about writing. Just write.

Writing is not fun when it's work. You turn it into work when you think too much about it.

Writing is not a problem to be solved. Writing is the grand adventure you (and your characters) embark on.

Writing is a paradox. It gives what you take. It takes what you give. It's powerful and makes you feel helpless. It's extraordinary and it's maddening.

If you commit to writing, you might find that the stuff you feel—rebellion, angst, worry, nervousness, fear—all of these emotions find a release when you start to write. The energy you feel in your daily life will come out in your scenes. And that's great.

You are investing yourself in your writing. When you learn to channel your feelings into writing, you will learn the true value of writing.

You might write a scene that helps you through a particular problem you were having that day. Writing is cathartic—it cleans out your emotions. It's like keeping a journal. Writing is also similar to going to therapy, where you get to share your feelings. Only you don't have to pay the eighty dollars or more an hour to your therapist. Writing a screenplay shouldn't make you freak out, pull your hair out, or bite your tongue. It doesn't have to be like that. Writing a script is not *that* overwhelming. You can write a script in a few days if you put your mind to it. You can write a script in several months, if that's how you choose to proceed. No matter how long it takes you, you need to *write.*

Start from the beginning. The first scene of your movie. That's all you need to worry about for now.

The very first scene.

How to Fight Writer's Block

There might be a time when you really *want* to write but nothing comes out. This is called writer's block. It's a lie; it doesn't exist. It is impossible to be creatively blocked. Your bowels could be blocked (and that's called constipation), but your creativity *cannot* be blocked.

If you have trouble finding things to write about, you have thrown up a roadblock in your creative path.

Get Out of Your Own Way

Start writing. *Anything!* So it's terrible. Who cares? *Write.*

You can delete or rewrite the crap later. Just move forward.

If you are truly having a difficult time writing, there's another possibility. You could be burned out. Maybe you need to take a break. This is called creative refueling.

You can't claim burnout unless you've actually been writing, though.

If you *have* been working on one project for a while and suffer a roadblock, you might be creatively exhausted.

Take a break. Writing one scene a day will *not* creatively exhaust you, so don't even try *that* excuse!

Write!

Fight the Critical Demon

People who are well versed in the English language sometimes have difficulty writing. These people spend a lot of time obsessing about whether their use of the English language is *perfect.* I don't know about you, but writing like that would drive me crazy.

Remember earlier when I talked about killing the critic? When you embark on your first draft, killing the critic is very important. The surest way to put up roadblocks for yourself is to become too analytical of what you have written.

The biggest trick to writing is learning to take advantage of inspiration when it hits and *not* worrying about the quality of what you are writing.

Some people can't do that. They overthink what they are writing and they become obsessive about writing perfectly. They usually don't accomplish much writing. Don't make this mistake.

Yes, you might write terribly. You may have misspellings, your grammar may be awful, and your characters might talk, talk, talk, and say nothing. It's all okay. First drafts are always butt-ugly. Just *get* a first draft! Do whatever it takes to get that first draft out of you.

Much as I wish I could, I can't write your screenplay for

you. You must now embark on your own journey for a bit. You must write your screenplay.

This is where real screenwriters who want a million dollars are separated from those who are interested in making a million dollars but not interested in doing the work.

Do the work. Write the first draft.

You will thank me for this swift kick in the butt later.

CHAPTER 5

If You Can't Do It, No One Can!

I promised at the beginning of this book not to load you up with screenwriting theory. You might have noticed that I *did* give you some screenwriting theory.

I lied. Sue me.

Here's my defense: the theories I provided were basic and hopefully were covered in a simple way.

If you follow the steps laid out in this book, you shouldn't have a problem getting to your first draft. If you don't feel ready to start your script, take some time and reread the previous chapters.

Then make sure you are working with the right concept.

Then make sure your story outline is tight.

Then reexamine your treatment.

Once you feel ready, it will be time to write your first script.

The following piece of advice is for the writers who are not afraid of writing a script and want to get their first draft out as quickly as possible.

Go, Go, Go . . .

Whip-snap. Ya! Write. Don't think. You already thought the story out in the treatment. Now *go!* Move it. *Faaaaster!*

Your first draft is going to suck total butt. Revel in its depravity. Wallow in its stench. Just get the darn thing out, and quickly. Pretend it's a demon and you need an exorcism.

Or think of this: do pregnant women casually birth babies when they feel like it? Heck, no. The baby comes and there is nothing anyone can do to stop it. You are giving birth to an infant. Pray it has ten fingers and toes. The most you can do, though, is push and hope for the best. When the nurse (your printer) puts the infant into your hands, *that's* when you cry tears of joy or sadness.

You'll probably think your baby is ugly. That's okay. It probably is. Birthing isn't pretty. It can be downright nasty!

When you're done with your first draft, put it away for a few days, hopefully a few weeks. You are exhausted. Take a break. Let creative mode slip away, and reconnect with reality mode.

This piece of advice is for writers who are frightened at the prospect of writing their first script:

Get Over Yourself

Your screenplay should be 80 to 120 pages long.

Your screenplay will have anywhere from 50 to 150 scenes (could be less, could be more).

There is *no* reason you cannot write one scene a day.

If you have developed your treatment, you pretty much know how many scenes will be in your movie. Therefore, you know how many days it will take you to write a first draft. Knowing that should take some of the pressure off. The trick is not to fall behind on your scenes. And if you do fall behind, make up the time you've lost. Write two or three scenes on a Saturday.

If you think writing one scene a day is too much, think of this: the average person speaks about 31,500 words per day. A normal scene is anywhere from 10 (short) to 10,000 (long) words.

Quit talking so much and write a scene instead!

And do *not* write one scene and then say, "I've exhausted my output; I'm done for a while." Write at least one scene *every* day. In no time, you will have a screenplay. It will be ugly; it will reek like the shoes you wear without socks. But it will be your very own first draft.

If you don't or won't believe you can write your first script, I can't help you along on your goal to making a million dollars. But thanks for buying the book!

SECTION FOUR

The Violent Art of
the Rewrite

CHAPTER 1

Becoming a Rewrite Warrior

Do you smell that? Whoo-ee, your backpack reeks.

What's that, you say? It's your script?

Are you sure something didn't crawl into your bag and *die*?

Seriously, I hope that if you're reading this chapter, it means you have a first draft of your screenplay. If you're still working on your first draft, there's no harm in skimming through the next chapters.

Before you start rewriting your script, make sure you've actually *finished* your script.

I know I can be demanding, but I know all your tricks. Don't try to get to the end of the process before you've done all the work.

Let's Say You Have a First Draft

While working on your first draft, you probably felt you were writing the most awesome thing ever. You probably had this excited message blinking in your head: "This is brilliant, this is brilliant."

That's cute. You were excited, in love with your words. You thought they were all perfect.

They weren't.

Pick up your script after a few days of not working on it. You will probably be like, "Where the heck did my brilliant screenplay go?"

The truth is your screenplay is somewhere between mediocre and brilliant.

Creating a story is a strange thing, and it's never very pretty. Remember how the process started? All the vomiting of ideas?

There is nothing pretty about vomit.

By writing your script, though, you vomited up a first draft. Even if it's stinky and filled with holes, good job.

Now it's time to start writing.

"What's that?" you ask. "Isn't that what I was doing?"

Well, yes and no.

The art of writing is not writing. The art of writing is *re*writing.

Finding Your Special Script

The reason screenwriting is open to all of us—English-language aficionados and amateurs alike—is because the real talent of writing is in the editing. Editing a script is not just about fixing spelling, punctuation, and grammar problems. In fact, the most important part of rewriting is fixing problems with content. Your descriptive passages and story, characters and their dialogue make up the bulk of the content in a screenplay.

Most of your time rewriting your script will be spent

fixing problems with descriptive passages, story, character, and dialogue. I realize you have spent so much time on your script that you think there must be *something* special there. There probably *is* something special there.

You just need to spend a lot of time finding it.

Rewriting Can Get Violent

During rewrites, you will beat the crap out your script until it gets better or you kill it (meaning you realize it's not a script worth working on anymore).

If rewriting sounds violent, that's because it is.

In fact, rewrite your script with a red pen. If you are twisted like me, you'll get a sick pleasure out of watching your pages bleed.

And you probably don't want to hear this, but I have to be up-front with you. Rewriting is a *huge* pain. It involves cutting up your script, tearing down scenes, rebuilding scenes, and ridding your script of anything that doesn't move your story forward. Then you repeat the process. Cutting, tearing, rebuilding, ridding.

And you repeat it again. And again. Again, again, again, again.

No matter how cool your story came out in your first draft, your script will need to be rewritten.

Just because you need to rewrite doesn't mean you are a bad writer. *Everyone* rewrites. The most important skill you will ever learn as a writer is how to rewrite.

Prepare Yourself for Battle

Rewriting your script is like hand-to-hand combat. You are the soldier. The script is your opponent. Your opponent will try to tempt you over to its side. It will lull you into believing your job is done and you can quit rewriting and relax.

Don't let your opponent fool you. Your script should be bleeding.

Cutting up your script is an instinctive thing, though. Rewriting, or learning what to cut and what to keep, is a skill that takes time and patience to learn.

Hopefully, the next few chapters will guide you through the process.

Rewriters Ready . . . Get Set . . . HALT!

Before we get going on the rewrite, there are a couple of important issues to discuss.

First, I have a little quiz for you:

You and your family share a disgusting dinner. Your stomach begins gurgling immediately. Your kid brother beats you to the bathroom, and he's in there for a while. You really have to go. He's taking his own sweet time. Finally, there's a flush and kid brother skips out of the bathroom, happy as a clam.

Do you 1) rush right in and do your business? or 2) give the room a little bit of time to *breathe*?

Unless you have a gas mask, I suggest going with the second option.

Give your script some time to become less offensive. If you are done with your first draft, put it away for a bit. You probably need to reconnect with the real world and take a break from writing. To approach your first rewrite, you need to be fresh and eager to go.

CHAPTER 2

The Bloody Battle Continues

Red pen in hand, you are a stealthy hunter ready to approach your rewrite. Ready to see some pages bleed.

What to cut? Where to cut?

Slow down, *Survivor* reject.

Before you start cutting, you need to get your wits about you. While much of what you have written in your first draft will be cut or rewritten, much is perfect the way it is. You need to learn what to cut and what to keep.

Get Some Input

We writers, if it were possible, would live in a creative vacuum. A creative vacuum is a great place where you get to be ultracreative with your writing and no one ever criticizes it—because no one ever reads it!

So if no one ever reads your script, how would you know you're ultracreative? Maybe you're just deluded?

Your script might be so special to you that you can't share it with other people. And certainly, it is too special to be *critiqued*.

But you don't have the luxury of writing in a creative

vacuum, not if you want to sell your work. You need other people to give their opinions about your script. Because let's face it—it's hard to judge your own writing. You will probably need other people's input about your script to figure out if you have fully realized your story and hit a bull's-eye or missed the mark completely.

You might feel that your first draft isn't ready to be seen. Perhaps you don't want to show it to anyone until you have gone through a few rewrites. That's totally fine. Whether you show a first draft to someone or wait until you've rewritten is a purely personal choice.

But let's pretend you're ready to receive feedback on your script.

Be Clear About What You Want

Many times in my writing career, I have given a script to family and friends. Sometimes it takes them months to read it. And when they finish, they'll call me up and say, "Nice job. It was great."

Not helpful at *all* in terms of helping me fix my script. It took me a while to learn that I needed specific feedback on my script to help me improve it.

To receive feedback that will help you improve your script, here's how to proceed:

1)   Pick three people whose opinion you trust.

2) Ask them if they have time to review your script. Tell them a script is not pleasant to read format-wise, but they should be able to get through it in two hours. Give them a two-week deadline.

3) If they can't commit to reading it in one sitting, ask someone else. You don't want people starting and stopping when they read.

4) If they commit to reading the script, ask them to review it for what it is, not for what it *isn't*. That means they don't compare the script to every movie they have ever seen. Also, let them know that it's okay to write comments on the script pages, but tell them not to worry so much about typos. If they find one, that's great, but you don't want them to read the script just to find all the typos. Make it clear that you need their help fixing story and character problems.

5) Prepare a list of five to ten questions that you would like them to answer *after* they read the script. Tell them to answer the questions honestly. Sample questions could include:
    - On a scale of 1 to 10 (10 being the best) how would you rate the story?
    - On a scale of 1 to 10, how would you rate the characters?
    - Were there any lapses of logic in the story?

- Was the lead character written in a believable way?
- (If your script is a comedy) Did you laugh out loud? If so, provide examples of the things that made you laugh.
- (If your script is a drama) Did the story touch you to the point where you felt emotionally connected to the script?

Ask any questions you want. Then ask the reader to provide general feedback about the script.

By approaching a script review in this way, you're setting a deadline and you're giving your reviewer an easy way to provide you with feedback. This, believe it or not, will take the pressure off you *and* the reader.

Suck It Up, Junior

The hardest part of receiving feedback on your script is hearing things about your masterpiece that you really don't want to hear. You asked for the feedback, though, so now you gotta deal with it!

No one will *ever* love your script as much as you do. Get used to that right now. Maybe you'll be told that your story isn't tight. Or the characters don't ring true. Or the dialogue is crappy. Or a certain scene doesn't work. (That hurts, particularly if it's your favorite scene.)

You will receive negative feedback about your script. That's unavoidable.

When someone criticizes your baby, your first instinct might be to scream, "You suck, loser!"

Chill. To become a writer, it is necessary that you learn to take criticism. You *can't* let criticism of your script make you angry or depressed.

Feedback on your script isn't meant to stroke your ego. It's meant to improve your script.

Don't take it personally.

The Power of Threes

Remember when I said you should give your script to three people to evaluate? This is a continuation of the mystery of the power of threes.

If you give your script to three people and one person liked a particular scene, another says the very same scene bothered them, and another says the scene was awful, whom do you trust?

You always trust what you have written. Always, always, always!

If you hear a criticism three times, though, you no longer trust what you have written. You trust the threes. If you hear three comments from different people about your script and the comments are similar, pay close attention. If three people read your script and they say the same thing—maybe that your lead character isn't interesting—you should *really* listen. If three people have the same or similar criticism of something in your script, they are right and you need to *re*write.

Zoetrope.com

If you don't have three people in your life who will read your script, there's another way to receive feedback.

Zoetrope.com is a free site for writers to share their work with other writers. This is a peer review site. After you review four screenplays posted on the Web site, you can post your script. Other screenwriters will then have the chance to review it. Again, it's free.

There are problems with the site, though. After you review four scripts and are allowed to post your script, there's no guarantee your script will receive *any* reviews for the thirty-odd days it's posted. And if you receive a review of your screenplay, there's no way of knowing whether the person who reviewed your script is qualified to do so (i.e., they could be a moron). The person could be cruel and rip your story even if it doesn't deserve it.

But if you get a few reviews and hear common criticisms about your script, you might learn about problems you hadn't considered. Remember the power of threes. If three people say the same thing about your script, you probably need to fix the problem they pointed out.

I recommend that you try out zoetrope.com, but be warned: you are dealing with many frustrated screenwriters who want to achieve the same goal as you. They want to sell a script. Many writers are on the Web site to improve their scripts, but just as many are there to make themselves feel better by belittling other writers.

Try the site out and see if you like it.

Familiarity Breeds Contempt

Before you start on your first rewrite, there is an important emotional concept I want to share.

You might need to break up with your script. You know—take some time apart. We all need breaks from things that take up too much of our energy! And this will happen with your script: you rewrite (hence reread) it so many times that you get sick of it. Writing something and then rewriting it repeatedly will make you want to vomit, and I'm not talking about ideas.

That's okay. When you see your written words so much, you get familiar with them to the point that you can't make sense of anything anymore.

If this happens to you, it's time for a break.

I often look at something I have written and get the creepy chills and scream, "Get away, get away, get *away*!" Then a few days later I'm like, "You are so *good*!"

Everything that once looked good will look ugly. Everything that once looked ugly will look good.

CHAPTER 3

The Good, the Bad, the Butt-Ugly

The rewrite process is the hardest part of screenwriting to teach, but it is, as I've explained, the most crucial aspect.

You will hopefully complete the rewrites in a step-by-step process that isn't too overwhelming.

The simplest way to approach your rewrite is to pick apart your scenes in a broad way. You will be looking at the big picture. That means you will look at your scenes in terms of how they relate to your story. You will spend a lot of time connecting your scenes to each other and the story. After you've done all that, you will tighten your script by dealing with smaller details, such as technical stuff and typos.

A Fresh Start

When you start your first rewrite, it's best if you haven't seen your script in a week. Maybe two. You need a fresh take on what you have written.

For the first read-through of your script before working on the rewrite, don't worry about typos. If you see one, it's okay to fix it. But there are more serious problems in your script than typos. Worry about the typos later. Remember, for this rewrite you will look at broad issues first, then specific issues. Story and character problems are broad. Typos are specific.

During this read-through, you are mainly looking for story and character problems. Particularly, you are looking to make sure everything that happens in your script makes sense. Is the story logical? Does one scene build to the next scene to the next scene to the next scene? From start to finish, does your script develop logically?

Make notes about your script, but don't necessarily start changing things yet. In fact, it's important to read your script all the way through to get a good sense of your story before making any edits.

Jot down notes about important story elements that need more careful attention, and then finish reading the script. Once you're done reading, let's take a closer look at your overall story. Is it linear or episodic?

Is Your Story Linear or Episodic?

Linear stories happen in a logical sequence and are told in a limited time frame. A week. Perhaps a school year.

Many teen movies cover the course of a school year. The story begins with the first day of school (or at the end of summer) and ends at the prom or graduation. A successful teen movie of the 1980s called *The Breakfast Club* took place in a very short amount of time—one day, during detention.

On the flip side, episodic stories may unfold over the course of a decade or more. With episodics, you can take a lead character from the age of one to age ten and then age twenty. Episodic stories may also switch more freely between past, present, and future than linear stories.

So which kind of story do you think would be easier to sell to Hollywood? Linear or episodic?

If you guessed linear, you'd be right on the money.

And which do you think is easier to write *well*?

If you guessed episodic, you'd be wrong.

You might be tempted to write an episodic story your first time out. It might seem easier in the beginning. First-time writers who write episodics usually don't have a firm grasp on linear storytelling. They write episodics simply because they cheat in their stories and go from past to present, one character to another, with no clear focus.

New writers rarely do episodics well.

Since you are new to writing, I suggest you write a linear story. If you have written an episodic, think about ways to make your story linear. And if you have written a linear story, think about ways you can tighten the story so it's told over the *least* amount of time possible. (Example: if your story is told over a two-year period, consider whether you can tell it over a two-week period.) That will give your story immediacy. Immediacy makes your story more engaging to the reader and, when your script is made into a movie, to the audience.

Why Do You Exist?

By now you have reread your script and made some notes and are ready to edit. So let's start with individual scenes.

The best scenes in your movie should accomplish one or all of the following: 1) reveal important information about a character and relationships, 2) provide information important to your story, and 3) present a conflict or two. At the very least, the scene should move your story forward.

Moving your story forward means there's information in the scene that's crucial to your plot.

Here's a tricky situation. Some scenes in a movie provide what I have referred to as color. Colorful scenes might be interesting but do not really advance the plot of your story. Should they be cut, or at the very least changed to fit the plot?

Yes. Even if it is brilliantly funny or creepy, scenes that are unnecessary to a story probably represent a tangent. A tangent is a scene or scenes that don't have much to do with your overall story. Going off on a tangent means you have taken a random direction with your story that's not important to your main plot.

If you find a tangent, perhaps you can turn it into a subplot. Review Section Two, Chapter 3, about subplots. A subplot, don't forget, needs to be relevant to your main plot. If you can't turn a tangent into a subplot or change the tangent to fit the overall plot of your story, whack the scene.

If you have a difficult time cutting a scene (or anything, for that matter) out of your script, then perhaps it *needs* to be there. For now. Perhaps the scene is important to the story; you just haven't figured out a way to make it connect in a logical way. Keep it. You have about nine more rewrites to go and can always cut it later.

Are you having trouble deciding if a scene is important? Ask yourself this: if you cut the scene, would the story make sense? If not, keep the scene for now. If the story makes sense without the scene, you know what to do.

Colorful Scenes Often Cover Plot Holes

If you have a scene in your movie that is colorful but doesn't advance the plot, you might be working with a scene that's covering a plot hole. A plot hole exists when the story stops making sense.

Are you trying to distract the audience from the fact that there's a hole in your story? Come on, be honest. A colorful scene might be interesting, but is it connected to the plot? If not, then a breakdown has occurred in your story and the colorful scene most likely is covering a plot hole.

If you see a plot hole, figure out where the logic in your story breaks down. Create a new scene (or scenes) that adds new information to your story to make it more logical.

Once you identify a colorful scene that does not have a purpose in the story, you will probably understand why the scene doesn't fit in your script anymore.

It doesn't feel organic.

The Cruelest Cut

You might stubbornly refuse to cut unnecessary scenes or story elements.

You have to be brutal with your script. You have to cut or reshape scenes you love if they are not important to the story. I call this the cruelest cut.

If you resist making the cruelest cuts, you should remember something. Your script, to be sold, must appeal to millions upon millions of people. You will not sell your script if it's filled with scenes only you or friends will appreciate.

If you don't care if your script sells, then rewrite the script any way that makes you happy. Keep all the scenes you love. You're the boss.

Even if you *don't* care if it sells, though, you still want to become a good storyteller. Don't you?

Unnecessary scenes or story elements will never appeal to anyone but you. So do us all a favor (yourself included) and whack or change unnecessary scenes or story elements. Because if you think about it, a script filled with a bunch of unnecessary scenes or story elements is flabby.

Do you want a fat script? *Do* you?

I didn't think so.

Ready for Liposuction?

It's often difficult to figure out if stuff in your script is interesting and relevant to your story. That's why it's helpful to receive feedback before you approach the rewrite. But if you are honest with yourself and remember that your story always needs to move forward, you will see that your script is filled with major flab and needs to be liposuctioned. You will remove unnecessary stuff from your script even if it hurts.

Take out your red pen and start cutting up your script. Or, if you are working directly on your computer, start deleting stuff (but always save a copy of your draft before making cuts, in case you cut something that needs to go back in later). Your goal is to turn your flabby little script into a physically fit street fighter.

For now, you should focus your attention on scenes in your movie that don't move your story forward. Cut them or reshape them.

It's all about the shape, baby.

If you're unsure whether to cut something, keep it for now. You'll tighten scenes later.

The Best Scenes Accomplish More Than One Thing

I hope you find scenes or other stuff in your script that do not belong or are in desperate need of a makeover. Why? Because it means you are critically evaluating your work. You recognize there are things in your script that do not push your story forward. Good job.

Perhaps, though, you have encountered a scene that *does* contain information important to the story. Just one little piece of information. If it's an interesting scene, keep it for now.

Remember, though: the best scenes serve more than one purpose. These scenes 1) reveal important information about a character and relationships, 2) provide information important to your story, and 3) present a conflict or two.

If your scene accomplishes just one of these things, you may not have found the most economical way to convey your idea.

Again, the best scenes serve many purposes. Yet if you reveal too much information in a scene, it might seem to the audience that too much is going on. There's a fine line between too much and too little information.

If you find a scene that exists solely to reveal one piece of information, you might want to kill that scene and figure out another place to put the information—obviously in another scene. This will force you to come up with some creative solutions. How can you make an existing scene work once you add a new piece of information culled from another scene you cut?

It's tricky. Just remember economy and recycling.

Shorter Is Better if It Means You Cut the Cheese

As you progress on your first rewrite, you should cut every major element in your script that isn't important to the story. Even if it hurts, you must cut it.

Don't be freaked out by the fact that your ninety-page script just became eighty pages. You will be expanding existing scenes and writing new scenes to fill plot holes. If you're working with the right story, you'll have enough pages to fill a script.

Your script should not be crammed with *filler* just because you're afraid you won't have enough material for a script. Filler is screenplay junk food. It fattens the script with empty calories. Empty calories tend to make you fart—a lot.

Cheese will do that too.

Essentially, your script is cheesy if it has too much filler. You need to whack filler, and you need to whack it even if you think you like it.

If something in your script doesn't serve the story, it doesn't belong in your script.

Simple as that.

So make your broad story changes and then save your script as a second draft. Take a break if you need to. Then it's time to move on to the next rewrite.

Get Your Flabby Scenes on the Treadmill

Scenes in your movie that are crucial to your story may still be flabby and need some trimming. The first step in rewriting your third draft is to look at each scene individually. You now want to tighten your scenes.

First, each scene in your movie should have a proper slugline. Make sure the slugline explains whether the scene takes place indoors or outdoors (INT. or EXT.), the location of the scene, and the time of day the scene occurs.

After that, the best way to approach a scene is to visualize it in your head. Look at each scene as if it were its own little movie. Imagine you are watching it in the theater. How's the pacing of the scene? Does it move too quickly or does it move too slowly?

A scene that moves too quickly usually has too much going on. Cut things if you need to make the scene clearer.

If your scene moves too slowly, the culprit could be too much filler. Whack the filler. Also, consider how you might spice up the scene. Add some color—as long as what you add makes sense to the plot or subplot.

Perhaps you need to rewrite the scene so that it accomplishes one or all of these things: 1) reveals important information about a character and relationships, 2) provides information important to your story, and 3) presents a conflict or two.

Get to the Point

For a scene to be effective, it should have a beginning, middle, and end. Again, this is not rocket science—the scene begins, something happens, and then the scene ends.

Each scene should start cleanly and with a purpose. And hopefully the scene is interesting. The scene should also have a conflict or two. It shouldn't ramble—action should take place. And the scene should end in a way that makes the audience want to move on to the next scene.

Let's look at an example of a not-so-great scene.

Jill intends to break up with her boyfriend, Freddy. Jill's a popular girl and Freddy is a total nerd. Jill and Freddy are at Jill's kitchen table doing homework. Freddy discusses a wild event that took place at the afternoon chess club meeting. Jill has no interest in the story, but she sighs and listens.

Freddy goes on and on. Then Jill turns to him and says they need to talk. After some fake tears, she says they need to break up.

If you have a scene like that in your movie, you have a sucky scene on your hands.

The scene should open like this: Jill and Freddy are doing homework, and Freddy jabbers on about chess club. Jill desperately tries to interrupt the dull story, but Freddy refuses to listen. He's avoiding the inevitable breakup.

Jill is bored to tears and screams:

JILL

Loser, listen. It's
over!

The scene is effective because it reveals important information about a character and relationships (Jill and

Freddy); it provides information important to your story (the breakup); and it presents two conflicts (Jill needs to break up but Freddy doesn't want Jill to break up with him).

The fact that the scene is short and sweet doesn't hurt, either.

In, Out, We're Done, It's Over

Your scene should get going right away. Very shortly after it starts, something needs to happen. Once a scene serves its purpose, get out of it as quickly as possible. It should end in a way that makes an audience interested in moving to the next scene.

As for ending the scene with Jill and Freddy, it's pretty much over when she breaks up with him. Sure, he's heartbroken, but he's probably not all that surprised. Freddy and Jill might have some words. Then the scene should end with him slamming the door.

You wouldn't want something like this:

Freddy leaves in a huff. Jill, upset, but happy to be free of Freddy, goes to the computer and IM's her friend Raquel to tell her she *finally* dumped the dork. Raquel is like, COOL, LET'S GO OUT. Jill writes back, SURE, I'LL MEET YOU IN YOUR DRIVEWAY.

Boring. The scene should be over once Freddy storms out of the room. Instead of having Jill IM her friend, instead cut to Jill as she taps on Raquel's bedroom window. Raquel comes to the window. Jill tells her about the breakup. Raquel is like, "Cool, let's go celebrate. Whoo-hoo!"

Then Freddy, who has been stalking Jill, runs over with a machete. . . .

After you start chopping up scenes in your movie (similar to what Freddy wants to do to his ex-girlfriend, Jill), make sure the scene gets going right away, something important happens in the scene, and it ends in a way that makes the audience want to move on to the next scene.

Tighten Your Descriptive Passages

Once you tighten each scene in your script, reread Section 3, Chapter 2. Because it's time to take another pass through your screenplay and tighten descriptive passages.

Little by little, during the rewrite of your descriptive passages, you need to be harsh. If a word doesn't need to be in your script, get rid of it. Tighten every descriptive passage in your script so that it is simple, visual, and necessary.

This is going to be a *huge* undertaking. You have no idea how much improvement your descriptive passages will need to make them simple, visual, and necessary. Fixing descriptive passages is a step you will repeat each time you rewrite your script.

Once you've tightened your scenes and descriptive passages, you've finished your third draft. As always, it might be a good idea to give yourself some space before moving on to the next rewrite. After you've taken a sufficient break from rewriting your script, it's time to start your fourth draft.

Round Four

DING, DING, DING.

> ANNOUNCER
> In corner number one,
> bearing a red pen and
> out for blood...
> Aspiring Screenwriter.

CHEERS from the CROWD.

> ANNOUNCER
> In corner number two,
> quaking in fear, Fourth
> Draft Screenplay.

The crowd BOOOOS!

Your poor screenplay. You just whacked it like a Mafia hit man.

How are *you* doing?

Probably a bit traumatized.

Learning to cut up your creative work is very unsettling. It almost feels evil, as if you've done something terrible to something that didn't deserve it. As you progress as a writer, though, you start to realize rewriting is a very important means to an end. You learn, over time, that the first, second, and third drafts of your script are not even *close* to the beautiful one you will end up with once all the rewrites are complete.

Okay, hopefully I've buttered you up enough for you to embark on the fourth draft.

Light at the End of the Tunnel

It's time to reread your script. Again.

You should be *feeling* your script, meaning that it's coming together and you're getting it. It still needs a lot of work. But do you see the light at the end of the screenwriting tunnel?

You might notice that previous cuts in your script have altered the story a bit and there are holes in your plot, or that they have left some scenes a bit confused. That's okay. Your fourth draft is when you clean things up. Connect the dots. Add stuff to clarify your story . . . but in a way that doesn't load your script up with too much exposition.

More Plot Holes—Jeez, Won't These Things Go Away?

As you read your script, you will probably get into your story. "This is so *good*!" Then, all of a sudden, something jars you. Something happens in your script and it doesn't feel right.

You have either encountered flab or a plot hole.

Before you try to whack the flab or fix the plot hole, make a note of the jarring incident and finish reading your script all the way through. Once you finish reading, it's time to start writing the fourth draft.

Fill It Up

Flab, we know, needs to be whacked or liposuctioned. Cut or reshape flabby scenes, or put important information in that scene into another scene.

Let's talk more about plot holes.

Plot holes occur when your story stops making sense. They are similar to potholes (the holes in the street that mess up your car's alignment). You're reading the story and everything is fine. Then, *boink*—something jars you. Plot holes are jarring because you realize your story has hit a bump. The story stops making sense for a bit. You're like, "*What* happened?"

Really what you should be asking is "What is *supposed* to happen?"

Filling in plot holes (and yes, you still have them and will have them for many rewrites to come) may mean that you need to write a new scene to make your story more logical. It may also mean tweaking an already existing scene so that it leads more smoothly to the next scene.

Here's another analogy: stories are like a string of blinking Christmas lights. Plot holes are the bad or burned-out bulbs that stop all the lights from blinking.

The fourth draft of your script is about removing bad or burned-out bulbs and replacing them with new bulbs.

It's all about the blinking Christmas lights, man.

Once Again, This Time with Feeling

To fix plot holes, usually you need to add information to a scene that helps the story flow in a logical fashion. You might need to create a completely new scene (or scenes). Whatever you need to alter or add to clarify your story, alter or add it now.

You should also cut any unnecessary stuff (yes, you left some during the previous rewrite) from your script. Anything that doesn't propel your story forward is unnecessary.

The process for your fourth draft then continues on the same path outlined for the second and third drafts:

1) Make sure the scene moves the story forward.
2) Make sure the scene has more than one purpose (reveals character and relationships, provides information important to the story, and features a conflict or two).
3) Make sure your scene gets going right away, something happens, and then you get out as quickly as possible.
4) Fix descriptive passages so they are simple, visual, and necessary.

If you haven't figured it out yet, writing a story is all

about providing information that leads us logically from one place to the next. Your job now is to make doubly sure that the information that makes up your story is told in a logical way.

You should also make sure the audience cares about your story. An audience will care about your story if they are invested in it. They will be invested in it if they care about your characters.

As you write your fourth draft, you need to pay close attention to your characters. Even more importantly, though, you need to make sure the lead character in your movie—the protagonist—is stellar.

I See You!

A movie audience expects to see the world through the protagonist's eyes. That means for two hours an audience is transported into a magical world, and they have a guide—your protagonist. Without a strong protagonist, an audience most likely will not be interested in your story.

It's okay to have a wimpy protagonist, at least in the beginning of your script. But at some point, the protagonist has to take control of the story and make things happen.

Remember, the audience wants to go along on your protagonist's journey. If your protagonist is not someone the audience enjoys watching, they certainly won't lose themselves in the journey.

So give your protagonist some kick-butt qualities and make him or her interesting.

Some Rules About Your Protagonist

Your protagonist should be in most of the scenes in your script. Scenes that don't feature the protagonist should relate in some way to his or her goal.

Here's an example. In *I.C.Q. (I Seek You)*, there are many scenes that feature the antagonists (Melanie's father and Victor's mother) conspiring to keep Melanie and Victor away from each other. These scenes relate to Melanie's main goal to win Victor Steele. The antagonists are trying to thwart Melanie in her struggle toward her goal.

Is your protagonist a dynamic force in your story, meaning they are crucial to the story?

If your protagonist *is* in most scenes but is not an active participant (meaning they are not making things happen), that's not good. You might need to give your lead character some oomph. Give them a more active role in the story.

Reevaluate your protagonist's involvement in the scenes. Does your protagonist have an active role in most every scene?

You might need to rewrite to ensure that your protagonist is the focus of the scene and the scene relates to either their main or smaller goals.

Once you take a close look at your protagonist, fix any glaring problems. Spend time on your fourth draft bringing your protagonist to the forefront of your story. Make sure the protagonist is the driving force.

Say What You Mean

Dialogue exists in a movie for many reasons. It allows the audience to get to know the characters, it allows characters to talk to each other, and it lets the audience know important information about the story.

Remember, the three major problems your dialogue will have are:

1) It is wooden or on the nose.
2) It contains too much information.
3) All the characters sound the same.

We've already discussed wooden and exposition-ridden dialogue, so let's talk about the characters in your movie sounding similar.

If the dialogue your characters speak sounds very similar, it's most likely due to the fact that they are pretty much all the same character. The easiest way to fix that is to change the characters in some way. Turn one character into the strong and silent type who takes action before speaking. Turn one character into an airhead. Turn another character into a genius. Change personalities or personas. Consider turning a character into an African American if they are white or a white person if they are Hispanic. Or a boy if they are a girl.

If you are not comfortable writing dialogue appropriate for a particular character, though, don't fall into stereotypes as to how you *think* certain characters speak. As star and executive producer of *Bringing Down the House,* Queen Latifah had to suggest changes to the original script's dialogue in order to ensure that a pivotal character's street slang seemed genuine.

Do some research and try to portray your characters' dialogue as genuinely as possible.

Once you adjust your characters, rewrite their dialogue to fit their new personalities or personas. Do the best you can to individualize your characters, but don't drive yourself crazy trying to make each character sound unique. Writing *good* dialogue is very important. Your characters may all sound the same (and often it's hard figuring out if they do or not), but it's okay as long as the dialogue is real, interesting, and important to the story.

As you progress with this rewrite, look for other problematic dialogue. Either make the dialogue sound more real or cut it altogether and find another way to express the information that's important to the story.

When in doubt, read dialogue aloud and ask how *you* would react to hearing it in a movie. If you cringe when you hear it, an audience will probably have the same reaction.

Sometimes Saying Less Is More

I have written many movies, and inevitably in each one a character goes *off* and has a full page of dialogue.

That's what is called a monologue.

Monologues are *not* good for screenplays. Big Fancy Hollywood Readers will hate them. "What *is* this? A script or a book?"

If the monologue is genius and fits the story, keep it. I am a huge advocate of letting your characters talk. But there *is* a point when there's too much dialogue. If you have a character and their dialogue runs for about six inches on the page, that's close to being a monologue. Make it shorter if you can.

Be Patient with Your Character's Development

Writing the fourth draft could take you some time. Go through the script scene by scene and tighten things up. Make sure each scene starts cleanly, has a purpose, and includes a conflict. Make sure each scene ends on a note that makes the audience eager to move on to the next scene. Tighten your descriptive passages to ensure that they are simple, visual, and necessary.

Your fourth draft will then be complete. Good job.

Take a break. You deserve it.

CHAPTER 4

Onward, Screenwriting Soldier

After a while, your script may become a muddled mess of words that has no meaning. You've seen your script too many times, and nothing makes any sense.

Perfectly natural.

Maybe you need some time away from it.

If you want to continue working on your rewrites, though, there's a way to overcome the problem of being too familiar with your script.

Stop looking at your script from beginning to end.

Spot-Check Your Script

If you've read your script so many times that you can't really see it anymore, the best way to begin your fifth rewrite is to review scenes randomly. This is called a spot check. Instead of reading your script linearly (one page after another), open up your script, pick a scene, and read. No longer are you worrying about story problems. You're looking at the scene completely independent from the story.

How does the scene work? Here's a good way to decide:

On a scale of 1 to 10, how interesting is the scene

(a rating of 1 being least interesting)? Be *honest.*

Go through your entire script and randomly rate scenes. When you're done, review the ratings. Why did you rate a particular scene the way you rated it? Did you give it a 2? That's a low number. That smells like a scene that needs to be whacked or changed. Did you rate it an 8? It must be a good scene. Why is it good? Does the scene move the story forward, reveal important information about a character and their relationships, and feature a conflict or two? Cool. You have an awesome scene.

Spot-checking and rating your scenes is a good way to evaluate them individually. This compels you to think of your scenes as separate components. Each scene should be able to stand alone. That means if a person were to read a scene, it would be interesting even if they didn't know what your story is about.

If you rate a scene 5 or below, you have a sucky scene on your hands. If *you* rate a scene low, how well do you think the audience will rate it?

If you rate a scene 6 or above, the scene is probably okay, though it still needs to be tightened.

Once you've spent time spot-checking your script, it's time to clean up more specific elements.

Flashbacks

There is a device occasionally used in scripts that I haven't explained yet, and that's for good reason: I don't want you to use it very often.

There's a chance you have already used this device, though, so you should learn how to use it properly.

A flashback is a story device you use when you stop your story and go back in time to reveal something that happened in the past. To be effective, flashbacks shouldn't be very long. They are snippets, brief moments that reveal something in a character's memory.

In *The Eruption,* my partner and I used a flashback to convey that the lead character, Christopher Hastings, has reached a decision. It's 1902, and Hastings is a photographer for *National Geographic.* His love interest is about to flee by boat from a city about to be wiped out by a volcano. Christopher knows that many people will die in the city if it's not evacuated. Safety is assured for him and the woman he loves, though, if he gets on a boat and sails away.

As Christopher prepares to get on the boat, a photograph of his father falls out of his bag. The photo launches the flashback.

```
EXT. THE BEACH — NIGHT

The beach is deserted. Christopher
paces along the shoreline, searching
the darkness for the boat.

                CHRISTOPHER
          They promised to wait!
```

                    SUZETTE
        Are you sure this is the
        place?

A boat appears through smoke that hangs
over the water.

                    HENRY
            Christopher! Over here!

The boat runs aground and Henry jumps
out. He helps Suzette into the boat.

                  CHRISTOPHER
            I'll push off.

Henry gets into the boat. Christopher
hands him his bag. The photograph of his
father slips out. Christopher notices it.

FLASHBACK:

EXT. A STUDY — DAY

Christopher is behind his camera.
Across from him is Chester Hastings,
who sits stiffly at a desk and looks
very unhappy.

                    CHESTER
          Aren't you done...
                    (flash)
          ... yet?

Chester blinks due to the flash.

                    CHESTER
          All that education
          wasted behind the back
          end of a contraption.

END FLASHBACK.

A flashback begins with <u>FLASHBACK</u> and ends with <u>END FLASHBACK,</u> as written in the preceding example. It means your story leaves the present and goes back in time.

If you decide your script could benefit from a flashback, use it wisely. And don't overuse the device. Big Fancy Hollywood Readers prefer that you not use flashbacks at all.

May I Ask Who Is Calling?

You might find that your script has a phone call or two in it. Phone calls provide a convenient way of telling parts of your story, especially now that most everyone has a cell phone. Phone calls can be incredibly boring. If you use a phone call in your script, make sure it's interesting. Check out the phone call at the beginning of the movie *Scream*. That's a genius phone call.

Phone calls in your script could be a sign of laziness on your part. Make sure there isn't a better way to provide the information. Perhaps the information told through the phone call could be revealed in a more visually interesting way.

If the call *is* important to your story, make sure the character talking on the phone is *doing* something interesting as they speak. The scene can't be static.

Songs and Sounds

Your script is probably filled with songs. I know this because I too was young and I remember how important music was to my life and to my writing. I used to write while listening to music, and I often found the *perfect* songs for many of my scenes.

Well, my friend, I have some bad news. You should whack any mention of songs in your script. There are many logical reasons for this. For one, the song that's superimportant to you will probably have *no* meaning to the person reading the script. Why waste space referring to it? Secondly, songs get old fast. You risk making your script seem out of date when you include songs.

The main reason you shouldn't use songs in your script is simple: beginning screenwriters use them a lot. You mark yourself as a beginning screenwriter if you refer to many songs.

If music is important to a particular scene, refer to it in a general way. Write something like this: Leslie and Jennifer enter the club to a BLAST of old-school house music.

Or

Hillbilly TWANG hits the unsuspecting HIGH SCHOOL-ERS, and they have no clue how to react to it.

BLAST and TWANG are written in all capital letters because they are sounds, and as I mentioned earlier in the book, sounds must be capitalized. Go through your script and make sure you have done that.

If you do use a song in your movie (and I strongly recommend against it), here's how you would write it up in your script:

MUSIC UP: PEOPLE ARE PEOPLE by Depeche Mode.

Or

PEOPLE ARE PEOPLE by Depeche Mode plays.

It's not a big deal how you do it, just make sure the name of the song is in all caps and you mention who performs it. Make sure it's essential to the script, though. If it's not, whack any reference to it.

Drafts Five Through Infinity

Your screenplay will continue to go through many rewrites. After draft five, remaining rewrites focus on fixing everything we have already covered. Work on as many drafts as you need until your script is so dang hot and so dang cool and so completely *explosive* that it's buzzing with its own energy. Review all the things explained in this and previous chapters and then rewrite your screenplay so that the story and characters are tight.

For your convenience, here is a list of some of the major things to consider as you continue to rewrite:

- Look for story and character problems.
- Ensure that everything that happens in your script is logical.
- See to it that each scene builds to the next scene to the next scene to the next scene.
- Tighten the story so it's told over the smallest amount of time possible.
- Double-check that your scenes reveal character and relationships, provide information important to your story, and present a conflict or two.
- Seek out and fill plot holes.
- Remove *anything* unnecessary in *every* scene.
- Make sure each scene has a proper slugline.
- Fix pacing issues.
- Check to ensure that each scene starts cleanly and with a purpose.
- End each scene in a way that leaves the audience wanting more.
- Fix descriptive passages to ensure that they are simple, visual, and necessary.

- Make sure subplots have a beginning, middle, and end.
- Strengthen the protagonist so he or she is a dynamic force in the story.
- Tweak dialogue so it's tight and not wooden, doesn't contain too much on-the-nose information, and sounds real.
- Avoid monologues.
- Spot-check your script.
- Use flashbacks correctly.
- Avoid phone calls.
- Avoid any mention of songs.

CHAPTER 5

The Polish

Let's pretend your script is close to being done. It's on fire—transcendent and magical. Nearly perfect in story and character.

If that's the case, it's time to start the polish. The polish is when you spit-shine your script. It's the last step you take before you start showing your script to Hollywood.

In the polish, you want to ensure that every component in your screenplay is the best it can be. Your descriptive passages. Your dialogue. The technical stuff like your sluglines and transitions.

They *must* be stellar.

Also, during the polish there are specific problems to focus on.

The Problem with "Its"

Polishing your screenplay means making final adjustments so that it sparkles. This is when you fix misspellings and common grammatical problems.

First, misspellings.

You have spell check. Use it. That's very simple. Spell check, though, can't find words that are spelled correctly but used *incorrectly*. In short, it can't find common grammatical mistakes.

So let's go over the most common grammatical mistake:

"It's" and "its."

No lie, this is the most common problem in a new screenwriter's script. You need to know the difference between "it's" and "its."

"It's" means "it is", as in it is a problem if you use the word in the wrong way. "It's" is a contraction of "it is" or "it has" and does not imply ownership or possessiveness. It's time to go to the movies. It's time to work on your screenplay.

It's been real.

"Its," on the other handy, is a possessive little creature. It implies ownership. Its hand went to her throat. The movie had its share of problems. The screenplay had its moments.

Go through each page of your script and fix problems with "it's" and "its."

Trust me, you have much correcting to do.

While "it's" and "its" will be the most common mistake, there are many others.

"Their," "there," "they're."

"Your," "you're."

"We're," "were," "where," "wear."

"Allusive," "elusive."

In short, don't assume that each word you write in your script is right. Read each word closely. The task in the polish is to go through your script—and this is a total pain—word for word and make sure all words have been used correctly. You'll be surprised to look up even simple words and realize you've used them incorrectly. To be safe, look up the meaning of every word you are unsure about.

Nixing the -ing

Another common problem in screenplays is the overuse of verbs that end in "-ing." She is walking to the door. He is holding the glass in his hand. They are riding the elevator.

What do those sentences tell you?

They tell you that there is a simpler, more dynamic way of showing action in a script.

She walks to the door. He holds the glass in his hand. They ride the elevator.

Fewer words.

Your script needs fewer words. Nixing the "-ing" makes your sentence more powerful.

Don't go crazy and remove every single "-ing" word. They are often needed. They just aren't as dynamic as a single verb that says the same thing in a cleaner way. Removing "-ing" conserves words and makes action more immediate. Rather than writing, "She is making coffee," write, "She makes coffee." Instead of writing, "He is going to the store," write, "He goes to the store." There's no need for a character to be walking, holding, or riding. Characters walk, hold, or ride. That will make action in your script more dynamic.

A Final Word About Too Many Words

I've said it before, but a script is a bore to read.

What makes a script even more boring to read? Words used incorrectly or unnecessarily. Make your words count. Use them correctly. Cut all unnecessary words. Spit-shine your script so that it's a joy to read.

Don't try to convince yourself that it's good enough. Polish the heck out of your script. It should be as close to perfect as you can get it. Remember your competition. Thousands of other writers are trying to sell their screenplays to Hollywood. Many of them spend tons of time polishing their scripts. You need to do that too.

You might be on your way to writing a script that is brilliant. But unless you spend the time rewriting your script, it will remain mediocre.

It is up to *you* to cross that line to brilliance.

SECTION FIVE

Getting Your Script to Market

CHAPTER 1

Attention, Shoppers

Your script is a masterpiece. No one has ever seen anything like it before. It's *explosive*. It's going to make us laugh. It's even going to make some of us cry like overgrown babies.

It's going to kick some serious butt.

Okay, so now what?

You are close to shopping your script to Hollywood.

Before you start shopping, though, you probably have a question. "What if someone rips me off?"

Many new writers feel that their work is very vulnerable to theft. They are afraid their brilliant script could be stolen from them. There is an itty-bitty tiny truth to this, but mostly it's writer's paranoia. Don't scare yourself. It's unlikely that your script will be ripped off.

However, it *is* a good idea to protect your screenplay before you share it with other people. Protecting your work gives you peace of mind that if you had to, you could prove that you wrote what you wrote.

Most writers protect their script by registering it with the Writers Guild of America (WGA). (You could also file a copy of your script with the United States Copyright Office, but copyrights are a bit complicated. For now, do what most writers do and register your script with the WGA.) To learn the process of registering your script, visit the Writers Guild Web site at www.wga.org.

Registering your screenplay with the WGA means you are placing a copy of your material in storage for five years. To register your script with the WGA, you can drop it off at their offices in Los Angeles or New York. If you don't live in either L.A. or the Big Apple, you can mail a hard copy of your script to the WGA. You can also register it online if you have access to a credit card. At the time of this writing, it costs twenty dollars to register a script.

If someone tries to rip you off, you can go back to the WGA and ask them to pull the original from storage. This will be your proof of when you registered it.

And it *is* worth the money, just for the peace of mind.

You Cannot Protect a Title or Concept

You can protect your script—your stories and characters and dialogue and the way you express your ideas. You cannot protect titles or story ideas (you know, your movie's concept?). This seems strange to many writers, but it's something you should know.

Say you write a movie called *Astronaut Boy* about the youngest astronaut ever to make it to space. Say you shop the script to Hollywood and no one buys it. Then, a year or more later, you read in the newspaper that a studio has come out with a movie called *Astro Dude,* and it's a movie about the youngest astronaut ever to make it to space! You'll be like, "Holy crap, they stole my movie!"

Well, maybe yes and maybe no. If it turns out *Astro Dude* has a very similar story and/or elements to the ones in your script, then quite possibly you were ripped off. That's when it might be time to hire an attorney, which could be expensive. In order to prove you were ripped off, though, you most likely would have to prove that someone connected to the movie similar to yours had access to your script—not always easy to prove.

However, if the movie that comes out has no real similarity to your movie (other than the title and/or basic concept), there's not a whole lot you can do.

Similar scripts are sold to Hollywood all the time. My writing partner and I shopped our volcano movie, *The Eruption,* and three other volcano movies sold in the space of a month. Stuff like that happens all the time.

The biggest danger of theft you will face is this: you send your script to someone in Hollywood and the person loves your story idea but thinks the script sucks. So they find a more established writer and pay them to write a script based on your story idea. I can't lie—that could happen, and it has. However, if you're too worried that someone will steal your idea, what ends up happening? You never send your script out. If you don't send your script out?

You never have a chance of selling it.

The best thing you can do to keep anyone from stealing your title and/or your concept is simple: don't shop your script until it's really, *really* good.

Here's why. Why would a producer steal your title and concept if your script is really good? There would be no point. They would simply buy *your* script.

Stealing stuff means a producer is this much closer to rotting in Hades. They do not want to rot in Hades. They would probably prefer not to steal things. The major reason a producer would be tempted to steal your story idea is they didn't like your script.

So write a really good script.

(Please note: if you ever shop a script to Hollywood and later think someone might have stolen your script or any part of it, seek legal advice. I don't mean to guide you in any legal way. Only a qualified entertainment lawyer can sort this out for you.)

CHAPTER 2

Beware the Salesman Bearing Snake Oil

Once you protect your script by registering it with the WGA, make sure it is good enough to send to Hollywood.

Some of you might be tempted just to run with what you have. To send it out and hope for the best. That can be a terrible mistake. If you shop a script too soon, you might blow your chance of shopping it later. In Hollywood, everyone wants to read the next hot thing. They don't want to read something that has been shopped all over town.

As you get ready to shop your script, you may hear about companies that offer to review your screenplay. And if they think it's good, they'll help you shop it to Hollywood. If it sounds too good to be true, that's because it is. You will quickly learn that it's extremely difficult to have your script read by anyone in Hollywood. And there are many, many companies out there that are more than willing to take your hard-earned cash by promising to help you.

Avoid the Money Pits

The most visible types of companies out there that claim to help sell screenplays are script coverage services. These companies offer to have your script read by a Big Fancy Hollywood Reader. If the Big Fancy Hollywood Reader likes your script, the script coverage service will shop it to Hollywood!

In reality, these companies take your money and all you get in return is coverage telling you why your script sucks.

Let me explain.

What the Heck Is Coverage?

Coverage is a two- to four-page analysis of your script. A Big Fancy Hollywood Reader writes the coverage. Script coverage services are not the only ones who employ Big Fancy Hollywood Readers. Agents, managers, producers, and studio executives also hire Big Fancy Hollywood Readers to analyze scripts for them.

At the end of the coverage written by the Big Fancy Hollywood Reader, usually one of two words appears: PASS or RECOMMEND. PASS means the Big Fancy Hollywood Reader has decided your scrip sucks and rates no further consideration. Most scripts that are covered in Hollywood receive a PASS. RECOMMEND means the script is worth further consideration. Very few scripts get this.

I have no doubt that there are many crappy scripts

floating around in Hollywood. Most of them deserve a PASS.

But I have learned firsthand why receiving coverage on your script is useless. One Big Fancy Hollywood Reader might say a script is terrible. Another Big Fancy Hollywood Reader may read the exact same script and say it's great!

Many years ago, I worked at a movie studio and I was able to submit my script for coverage. I didn't even have to pay for it. I also had friends at other studios, so they submitted my script for me as well.

The script was *Little Girls,* the one I cowrote with my partner, Shannon. The script went for coverage at three major film studios.

When I got the coverage back, it was disturbing. Not because I can't take criticism. My skin, much to the chagrin of my dermatologist, is very thick. I was disturbed because the coverage from two studios said the script was terrible. Keep in mind, *Little Girls* was a script that had already gotten me two agents, so I knew it wasn't bad. The Big Fancy Hollywood Reader from the third studio, however, gave the script a NO—SEE COMMENT. This uncommon rating falls between a PASS and a RECOMMEND. NO, I can't recommend the script, but SEE COMMENT because there's something worthwhile in it. The Big Fancy Hollywood Reader felt the script was well written and had potential.

The same thing could happen if you submit your script

to a script coverage service. Their Big Fancy Hollywood Reader might hate your script.

Ouch, that just cost you a lot of money to be told your script sucks. Eighty dollars or more.

You could take a chance and submit your script to another coverage service. But it's gonna cost you another eighty bucks.

Finding a Big Fancy Hollywood Reader who actually likes your script could cost you a lot of money!

Script coverage services are not *totally* useless. They *do* shop scripts that receive a RECOMMEND to Hollywood. In addition, they have had *some* success selling scripts. Not much, though. Do you really have the money to fork over to take that chance?

If your script is good enough and you shop it to Hollywood properly, you won't need script coverage services. Your script *will* find its way into the hands of someone in Hollywood who will help you.

So please, think twice before you pay companies to read your script.

From $450 a Week to a Quarter Mil

Many people in Hollywood say that the best way for a young writer to be noticed is to win a screenwriting contest.

Uh, okay.

Winning contests is not very easy. Everyone and their brother are trying to win contests. It costs money to enter—twenty dollars and up. Also, you usually have to submit a copy of your script (which costs money to make) and send it via regular mail (which also costs money). You have to fill out registration forms (which takes time). Signing up for contests can be a pain.

Yet if you were to win a particularly well-known contest, great things *could* happen for your career.

I knew a young woman who won a prestigious screenwriting contest. She went from being a receptionist who made a few hundred dollars a week to making a quarter of a million bucks in a very short amount of time. She signed with William Morris Agency (one of the biggest agencies) and has since become a millionaire.

That was over a decade ago.

There are only a few screenwriting contests with that much prestige anymore. If you win or place high in a screenwriting contest, though, you may get requests from people in Hollywood to read your script.

So, if you have the time and the cash, consider entering some contests. To learn more about them, check out one of my favorite screenwriting Web sites, www.scriptsales.com.

Be Creative

I have talked about script coverage services and contests as tools you might be tempted to use to see if your script is good enough to shop to Hollywood. If you really want to know whether your script is ready to shop, don't spend money on script coverage services or contests.

Hello! Be *creative.*

Hook up with a local theater group and ask the literary manager or director to help you perform a live reading of your screenplay. Live readings don't have to be acted out. Actors sit on a stage and simply read your script. A narrator reads your descriptive passages. Invite anyone you can think of to your reading. Afterward, provide the audience (and the actors) with an evaluation form requesting a rating from 1 to 10 on issues important to you regarding your script. After you have tallied up your evaluation scores, you should have some clear answers about the quality of your script. Is it ready to shop to Hollywood?

You might think that a live reading will be difficult to pull off, but it's not. Your local theater group will help you in a second. The most difficult part of a live reading isn't putting it together but sitting through it. Hearing actors read your dialogue might be painful! It could show that you have a lot of work to do.

On the other hand, a live reading could provide a very low-cost and extremely useful way of helping you decide if your script is ready to shop.

Oh, and before you shop to Hollywood, go through your script one last time. Do *one* more rewrite.

Groan, I know. Just do it. Try to be honest with yourself and spend the time you need to make your script as close to brilliant as you can get it. If you think it's ready . . . if you truly believe in your heart it's ready . . . it's time to pitch your script to Hollywood.

CHAPTER 3

Shop Till You Drop

Did you know there *is* no Hollywood?

There *is* a city named Hollywood, and I once lived in it. Just a few blocks shy of Hollywood and Vine. But "Hollywood" as most people know it is a metaphor for the movie industry.

The truth is *no* major movie studio (to which you would *love* to sell your script) is actually located *in* Hollywood. The major movie studios are located in Culver City, Burbank, Santa Monica, and Universal City. (Technically, all these cities are in Los Angeles.) "Hollywood" is an illusion. This is important only because I want you to start thinking of the creation of an illusion.

Did you know that most hot actors and actresses are geeky people just like you and me? The difference is that most hot actors and actresses have a whole staff of people helping to create the illusion that they are fabulous, important, and powerful.

You need to create the illusion that you are a new and hot writer and your script is the *next big thing*. Your goal is to make anyone who hears about you and your script say, "Get me that script. I *have* to read that script!"

You must create your own hype. That means you are going to create the illusion that you are a writer who deserves—no, who *demands*—a million bucks from "Hollywood."

How do you do this? Well, you need a good, if not great, script. No amount of hype will help you turn a poorly written script into a hot commodity.

If you have a really good or great script, then next you need to confidently and professionally pitch it to Hollywood. Pitching means submitting your script or telling someone about your story.

Before I talk about how to pitch your script, I want to talk about the people you'll be pitching to. The two most obvious groups of people are literary agents (agents) and literary managers (managers).

Agents

Literary agents are people who sell screenplays to Hollywood buyers. The buyers are usually producers (the people who put together movies) or movie studios (the companies that make movies).

There are hundreds, if not thousands, of literary agents throughout the country. Most agents work at agencies. The huge agencies are ones like William Morris Agency (WMA), Creative Artists Agency (CAA), and International Creative Management (ICM). Those agencies are hard to get into as a young writer. Not impossible, but very difficult.

Usually, you will want to pitch your material to a small or midsized agency. Regardless of its size, the agency should be located somewhere in Los Angeles.

The literary agent should also be what is called WGA signatory. Remember the WGA, the place to register scripts? Well, the WGA is a union for writers. WGA-signatory agents or agencies are ones the WGA has deemed reputable. To find a list of WGA-signatory literary agencies, visit www.wga.org and click on List of Agents. Then find the list of agents located in California.

The agencies in Los Angeles are the agencies you will be targeting for a pitch. Targeting for a pitch, by the way, simply means you will be sending letters to these agencies. We will cover this more later.

Print a list of WGA-signatory agencies and become familiar with them. There won't be any agents listed, just agencies. That's okay for now.

Literary agents are a natural place to shop your script. After all, that's why they exist, right? To sell scripts? But literary agents are increasingly difficult to reach. Honestly, most of them are *not* looking to develop a relationship with a young, promising writer. Agents want to work with someone who is already making money. It sucks, but it's the truth.

I know a guy who sold a script. The script was made into a movie (that's pretty rare, by the way—most sold scripts are *never* made into movies) and he *still* had a hard time getting an agent.

Again, agents are difficult but not impossible to land. If you have the right material and can create the illusion that you are a hot new writer and your script is the *next big thing,* you just might be able to do it.

Let's just say you do land an agent. What happens next? Usually the agent will sign you to a contract that stipulates they will represent your work (that is, your script) for a certain period, and if your script is sold, they will receive a 10 percent commission of any money you make. Therefore, if you sell your script for $250,000, your agent will get $25,000. That leaves you $225,000.

If you were only so lucky.

Managers

Besides pitching to agents, you may also pitch your script to literary managers. Managers are different from agents in a couple of major ways. Many managers today exist in a role that is a combination of agent and movie producer. They also help develop your career as a writer. That means they might help you develop your script. Then, when your script is ready, they'll help you shop it. If the script is purchased and made into a movie, the manager might also become a producer of the movie.

Many managers *will* take time to help a young writer develop a script and/or their career—*if* they feel the writer has very strong potential to sell a script that will be turned into a movie.

I mentioned that agents might sign you to a contract for a short amount of time. Usually you can get out of a contract with an agent if they haven't sold any of your work within a certain time period (say a month or two). Managers, however, will probably want to sign you for a lengthier amount of time. Say two years. They will tell you that it takes time to develop a writer's career and they need to protect their investment. And they make a strong point. It may take a long time to develop a young writer's career. So two years is reasonable on one hand, but a bit of a gamble on the other. If you are not happy with your manager and there is no way to get out of your contract, you will be stuck with them for two years.

Legally, a manager *cannot* sell your script. If you're

signed with a manager and they share your script with a buyer and it looks like it will be sold, your manager will hook you up with an agent (or possibly an entertainment lawyer, but let's stick with an agent) who will technically make the sell.

This is where it gets interesting.

Remember, agents take 10 percent of the money if your script sells. Managers take a heftier sum—usually 15 percent. That's 25 percent of your money. Let's say you sell your script for $250,000. Your manager and agent will get $62,500. You get $187,500. That's before taxes!

If you sell a script through a manager, it's very likely that you'll end up with *less than half* of the money you get for selling your script.

Here are some things to consider, though.

If you sell your script and your manager is a producer on the movie, the manager will usually waive their 15 percent commission fee because they will be receiving money to produce the movie.

Also, think of it this way: 50 percent of nothing is nothing. Even if you end up with less than $100,000 on a script that sold for $250,000, you have *more* than when you started out.

The truth is that managers are becoming increasingly important in selling scripts to Hollywood. You will probably have far *more* luck getting a manager to read your script than you will an agent. Managers are more willing to read the work of new writers because they have a lot to gain (15 percent and/or producing credit on a movie) if they find a hot new writer and the *next big thing.*

Be cautious, though. Literary managers are cropping up all over the place. Just about anyone can become a manager if he or she wants. *Never* give your literary manager any money. No reputable manager (or agent) in Hollywood will *ever* ask for money from you. They *may* ask for copies of your script so that they can send it out without having to pay for the photocopy charges. If they ask for anything more than that, don't walk.

Run.

The Producer and Studio Executive

I don't want to give you the impression that you must absolutely have an agent or manager to shop your script to Hollywood. You can always try to get your script directly to the buyers. Buyers, if you remember, are usually producers or movie studio executives.

Let's talk about producers first.

A producer is the person who puts a movie together. It could happen like this: the producer finds a script and gets a hot actor, actress, and/or director attached to the project (meaning that person agrees to be part of the movie). Then the producer takes the whole package to a movie studio executive, who works at a company that makes movies. "Here's your next hit movie. Greenlight the sucker and let's get going." Greenlight means a powerful executive at a movie studio gives a big thumbs-up to the whole package and agrees to spend millions of bucks to make the movie.

Alternatively, the producer may have a deal with a movie studio whereby the studio allows them to buy scripts. When the script is purchased, the producer works on packaging the movie.

However it works, the producer is a very valuable person in terms of setting up projects. If you get your script to a producer and they love the material, they just might be able to help you get your script directly to a movie studio.

Big producers usually have production companies, which are like mini–movie studios. They can be harder to reach. Getting in contact with a relatively new or up-and-coming producer can actually be easy.

I approached an up-and-coming producer with a pitch for my script *The Eruption,* and he was eager to read it. Little did I know he had just set up another volcano-related movie at a studio. He was checking to make sure the volcano movie I wrote would not compete with the volcano movie he sold.

Producers will do that. They want to see what else is on the market. They want to make sure the movie they just sold will not be facing any serious competition.

Producers are also in the business of bringing the freshest material to Hollywood. If you have a script that sounds interesting, they will want to read it.

Producers are usually looking for very specific kinds of

scripts. They know the genre they're looking for, they know the actor(s) they want material for, and they know the budgets they are working with. Regardless, they are definitely worth approaching.

As for movie studio executives, I recommend that you first try to get your material to an agent, manager, or producer. That being said, I have gotten meetings at movie studios by simply sending an e-mail directly to a movie studio executive. It's unusual to get those meetings without the help of an agent or manager, but it is possible.

Here's how I got my meeting at Disney.

I sent a pitch letter to someone who I knew was not the proper contact for a pitch. Let's say his name was John Doe and he worked in production. Mr. Doe e-mailed me back with the name of the person to whom I should send my pitch. I then sent a pitch to the correct person and was able to say that John Doe referred me. Having this referral helped get my e-mail read.

This brings up an important lesson. Most people in Hollywood like to work on a referral basis, meaning they prefer to take a pitch from a writer who comes to them through a referral from someone they know and trust.

You need to figure out how to get those all-important referrals.

Get Referred by Someone—It Totally Helps

Right now you should think of any- and everyone you know of who might be able to get you a referral in

Hollywood. If you don't know anyone directly in Hollywood, do you know anyone who knows someone who knows someone in Hollywood? *Anyone?* Maybe your sister is married to a guy whose cousin works in makeup at one of the studios. That's a contact. You need to work that contact. Ask your brother-in-law to put you in touch with the cousin. Once you contact the cousin, ask him or her to help you get your script to someone, *any*one in Hollywood.

Here's another crafty thing you can do to get yourself a referral.

Once, when I was looking for an agent, I did research on the Internet. I came across an old article written by an agent, and I really liked how she thought about the movie industry. I did a Google.com search on her name and found her name listed on a personal Web site for a young film director. His agent was the person I wanted to pitch. I didn't know this young director at all, but I sent him an e-mail. I told him about my successes as a writer and about my newest script. I also explained I was interested in his agent and asked whether he recommended her or not. The guy wrote me back explaining he really enjoyed working with the agent and that I should definitely send her a pitch letter. I e-mailed him and asked if he would feel comfortable initiating the process of introduction. He said he was happy to do so. The agent sent him back a reply saying I was welcome to contact her directly.

When I sent my e-mail to the agent, I mentioned in the subject heading that her client had referred me. Then, in the body of the e-mail, I sent her my pitch.

I've been working with that agency for a number of years now.

Even if you don't have contacts in Hollywood, with a little ingenuity you can create your own referrals. It doesn't always work—but why not try?

Unsolicited Scripts

Many times when you approach an agent, manager, producer, or movie studio executive, they will flat-out refuse to read your script. "We do not accept unsolicited material." That means these people have a policy of not reading anything they have not requested to read.

Or does it?

Just about everyone in Hollywood will say they do not look at unsolicited material. It's not always true. I would never have gotten meetings at Disney, Twentieth Century Fox, or other companies if I believed their policy of not accepting unsolicited material. If you reach the right person in the right way and they like your idea, you might get them to read your script.

It's Brighter than You Know

In my history as a writer, I have had four agents—one at a small agency, two at middle-sized agencies, and one literary (book) agent. I was signed with the top manager in Hollywood, the guy who did *American Pie.* I've gotten my scripts read by many producers who have done major hit movies. I've also gotten pitch meetings at movie studios with no help whatsoever from an agent, manager, or producer. All this I pretty much accomplished without having any major credits to my name.

Things can happen for you in Hollywood with the right attitude and, more importantly, the right approach. Most of my successes in Hollywood have been achieved with one simple thing. That simple thing is a stellar pitch letter.

CHAPTER 4

The Art of the Pitch

When trying to interest people in reading your script, you can't walk up to an agent, manager, or producer, fling a script at them, and hope it sticks. The laws of gravity, as well as the laws of California, don't allow such a thing. To get an agent, manager, or producer interested in your work, you must first pitch them your story.

The Pitch Letter

Before you send your script to an agent, manager, or producer, you must first send them a letter asking if they are interested in reading your script. This is your pitch letter, also called a query or query letter.

A pitch letter briefly sells you *and* your script. This is where you create the illusion that you are a hot new writer and have written the *next big thing.*

There are three main features of a good pitch letter:

1) It sells you.
2) It sells the script.
3) It's short and sweet.

I sent the following pitch letter to about sixty people. Fifteen people in Hollywood requested my script. That's a great response. You're lucky if two or three people out of sixty request your script.

So let's look at the letter and see why it worked.

Sample Pitch Letter

Today's Date

Mr./Ms. XX
Company name
Address
City, State ZIP

Re: *The Disposable Bride*

Dear Mr./Ms. XX:

I am the author of the five-book Camy Baker series published by Bantam Skylark, which sold close to half a million copies. I also cocreated a TV show at Fox Family Channel called *The Deal with Jenny Shields* that was in development for a year and a half.

I am currently seeking representation for my newest spec entitled *The Disposable Bride,* an edgy romantic comedy that has never been shopped.

The Disposable Bride

It's Valentine's Day in Los Angeles, and lonely Julie Dugan has all but given up on romance. But a terrifying encounter with a would-be stalker sets off an unlikely chain of events that leads Julie to the man of her slightly off-kilter dreams. (An urban *Romancing the Stone*.)

I was signed a few years back with Broder Kurland Webb Uffner for my spec *Little Girls,* which went out on a weekend read and received attention from Miramax and Stampede Entertainment.

I was also signed with Writers and Artists for my Fox Family Channel deal. My book agent is the XXX in New York. I currently have no film/TV representation.

I really believe *The Disposable Bride* has a unique voice with a very engaging lead character. Thanks for your consideration and please let me know if you'd be interested in taking a look at the script.

Sincerely,
Colton Lawrence
phone number/e-mail address

Okay, I had some advantages in this pitch letter. I was able to point to past successes as a writer. Yet I have sent out a similar letter where I pitched a different story.

Zilch. Nothing. Not one single request for the script.

The reason *The Disposable Bride* received so many requests to read the script was the combination of a catchy title and an interesting idea for a movie. The title and concept of the movie are key to a successful pitch letter. No matter how interesting you sound as a writer, people in Hollywood won't waste their time requesting your script if they don't like the title and, more importantly, the idea for your movie.

Let's Take a Step-by-Step Look at the Pitch Letter

Today's Date

Mr./Ms. XX
Company name
Address
City, State ZIP

Re: *The Disposable Bride*

Dear Mr./Ms. XX:

Always put the date at the top of your letter.

Then, no matter how you send a pitch letter (via e-mail, fax, or snail mail), always address it to a person and include their company's name and address. More on how to obtain names and addresses in a bit.

Under the address, put Re: and then the title of your script.

If you are sending this pitch letter via e-mail, make sure to include the script title in the subject line.

> I am the author of the five-book Camy Baker series published by Bantam Skylark, which sold close to half a million copies. I also cocreated a TV show at Fox Family Channel called *The Deal with Jenny Shields* that was in development for a year and a half.

This provides a brief introduction of my background as a writer.

> I am currently seeking representation for my newest spec entitled *The Disposable Bride,* an edgy romantic comedy that has never been shopped.

This explains that I am looking for an agent and introduces the title of the script (or spec) I am pitching. I also explain the genre of my movie and that the script has never been shopped before. This is important. Remember, no one wants to read a script that's been heavily shopped.

> *The Disposable Bride*
>
> It's Valentine's Day in Los Angeles, and lonely Julie Dugan has all but given up on romance. But a terrifying encounter with a would-be stalker sets off on unlikely chain of events that leads Julie to the man of her slightly off-kilter dreams. (An urban *Romancing the Stone.*)

This is my title and logline. A logline is a short description of my script. It's similar to the concept (remember those?) of the movie I came up with before writing the script.

In parentheses, I also included a reference to an old movie to which *The Disposable Bride* is somewhat similar. For instance, if your movie is about illegal speedboat racing, you could say it's like *The Fast and the Furious* on water.

> I was signed a few years back with Broder Kurland Webb Uffner for my spec *Little Girls,* which went out on a weekend read and received attention from Miramax and Stampede Entertainment.

I was also signed with Writers and Artists for my Fox Family Channel deal. My book agent is XXX in New York. I currently have no film/TV representation.

These two paragraphs provide a bit more information about me as a writer. Of course, this part isn't necessary if you don't have anything to add.

I really believe *The Disposable Bride* has a unique voice with a very engaging lead character. Thanks for your consideration and please let me know if you'd be interested in a taking a look at the script.

A brief wrap-up.

Sincerely,
Colton Lawrence
phone number/e-mail address

Don't forget to provide your contact information. If you're sending a pitch letter via e-mail, then it's not as important. The person can always respond to your e-mail. If you're sending a letter by fax or snail mail, however, the person needs some way of contacting you!

May I See Your ID, Please?

If you don't have any experience as a writer or have never won a screenwriting contest . . . tell them your age.

A twelve-year-old writer with a cool and professional pitch letter? Most agents, managers, and producers will want to read the script if they also like your title and concept. Discovering a hot twelve-year-old writer would be stellar for their career. Think of the media attention! MTV News profiles a twelve-year-old from Peoria who sold her script to Hollywood—and made bank!

Because of the Riley Weston fiasco, though, agents, managers, and producers will probably want some sort of verification that you are who you say you are before they fall in love with and then buy your script. You might have to send them a copy of your school ID or something.

Just joking.

There *is* a cutoff when I think age becomes less special in a pitch letter. I would say that in Hollywood that age is twenty. If you're under twenty, mention your age in the query letter. If you're older than that, don't refer to your age. There's no rule here, that's just my opinion.

If you don't have anything other than credentials or age to refer to, get to the point: sell your script.

Sell it hard.

To sell your script hard, you need to have a sparkling logline.

Make Your Logline Stellar

Remember, a logline tells what your movie is about in a few sentences:

> It's Valentine's Day in Los Angeles, and lonely Julie Dugan has all but given up on romance. But a

terrifying encounter with a would-be stalker sets off an unlikely chain of events that leads Julie to the man of her slightly off-kilter dreams.

Remember earlier in the book, I said you need a sparkling concept before you write the script?

Now you know why.

Without a good concept, what the heck are you going to talk about in your pitch letter? To get someone in Hollywood to read your script, you need a great logline.

Loglines can be very similar to the concept you came up for your movie. However, you probably need to tweak the concept a bit to make the logline even better. A good logline tells a brief story: a likable person or persons overcome(s) someone or something to win something important to them.

Try not to write your logline in one long sentence. You don't want to cram all the stuff in your story into one line. At the same time, don't make it too long. It must be simple, to the point, and interesting.

If I have to think twice about your logline, I am not going to think twice about your logline.

Marketing Is a Blast—Not

After you prepare your pitch letter, start making a list of all the people in Hollywood who can help you sell a script.

You know what a player is, right? Players make the game happen. Your pitch letter should go to the players in Hollywood, whether they are agents, managers, producers, or studio executives. To get a pitch letter to a player, you need to know their name, address, phone number, fax number, and e-mail address.

Finding information about players is easy . . . if you have money. There's a set of books called the Hollywood Creative Directory, which lists agents, managers, and producers and production companies. You can buy the books or use the Hollywood Creative Directory online. Both cost a lot of money.

If you have the money, great. Get the books or use the service online. It will make it easier to find contact information. If you don't have the money, it's still possible to get contact information for the players in Hollywood. It just takes a *lot* of research.

Start Reading Any- and Everything You Can Find About Hollywood

I love www.scriptsales.com. Not only does it provide great information about screenwriting contests, but it also lists scripts and other properties that have been sold to Hollywood. Go through this list. Often the list of sales will include agents/managers/lawyers who sold a particular property, along with the producers/production companies/studios that bought it.

These are the players in Hollywood. These people are selling and buying things in Hollywood. Write all the names down. After you find names, get onto the Internet and figure out how to contact these people. Ultimately what you need to do is create a database of people in Hollywood to whom you can send pitch letters.

Building a database isn't easy. I hope you're technically savvy and know what I mean in terms of building a database. If not, find someone to help you.

To build a database, you need the names of players in Hollywood and you need their contact information: where they work, their address, their phone number, their fax number, and their e-mail address.

The best way to contact a player, by the way, is by e-mail. E-mail addresses are hard to find, though. Faxing letters is second best. If all else fails, send your pitch letter via snail mail.

A great place to find contact information for people in Hollywood is www.inhollywood.com. I like it because it lists plenty of e-mails. As of this writing, you can sign up for a free two-day trial period.

Before you sign up for the two-day trial period, do your online research and collect as many names of players you can find. Then sign up and track down as much contact information as possible in those two days. If you like the service and can afford it, you can pay to join the site after your free days are up. Like the Hollywood Creative Directory, though, it can be expensive.

Another place to get free information about players in Hollywood is www.imdb.com. This Web site provides movie credits. Credits are a list of the people who worked on a movie. You will find names of producers and production companies associated with every movie Hollywood releases. If you want to find contact information for the producers and production companies, along with a lot of other useful information, sign up for a two-week trial period at www.imdbpro.com. As of this writing, it's free to sign up, but you need a credit card.

Another great way to gather contact information for Hollywood players is by asking your fellow writers for tips in screenwriting chat rooms and on message boards.

Regardless of how you get the contact information for your players database, start reading any- and everything about Hollywood. Most people in the movie industry read the *Hollywood Reporter* (www.hollywoodreporter.com) and *Variety* (www.variety.com). If you can't afford to buy subscriptions to these magazines, at least read as much information as you can online. These two resources provide invaluable information about the players in Hollywood.

Write down the names of players when you see them. Then do massive amounts of Internet research to track down their contact information. In this way, you become familiar with the players in Hollywood.

Cool Screenwriting Software You Might Want to Invest In

I've said before that I don't think young screenwriters should spend a lot of money on screenwriting. That's the beauty of screenwriting—you don't need much to write a script. Yet you probably already understand that marketing your script is a huge pain.

There is nifty software available to help you market your script. It's called Power Tracker, and it costs about eighty dollars. This software comes loaded with the names and contact information of five thousand people in Hollywood.

The contact information provided in my version of Power Tracker was not up to date. As of this writing, the software developer says they are working on a feature that will allow you to get one free update to your contact list when you purchase your software. One other slight problem with the software I tested was that it didn't list many e-mail addresses, mainly just addresses and phone and fax numbers.

Just the same, Power Tracker is a very cool database of Hollywood players. In addition, you can update information about players on your own. Say you find a certain player's e-mail address. Cool; type it into the database. It's quick and easy.

Power Tracker is more than a database—it also helps you generate pitch letters and allows you to keep track of any letters and scripts you send out.

I highly recommend Power Tracker. It will save you a lot of hassle when you begin marketing your script to Hollywood. (I am jealous I didn't have this software when I was pitching my scripts!)

Hang In There

It will take you some time to compile a list of agents, producers, and managers. Once you have your database of players, you are ready to send out your pitch letter.

To send out a pitch letter, you need some skill on the computer. Not only do you need to know how to create a database, but you also might want to learn how to do a mail merge. A mail merge allows you to take names from a database and merge them into a form letter. Once the merge is complete, you will have letters for each of the people in your database without having to type in each letter separately

If this is a foreign concept to you, find a technologically gifted friend, sibling, or parent who can help you.

Unfortunately, things get even trickier.

Say you have a list of players and all you have is their snail mail address. So you have to write letters to each of them. (This is where mail merge becomes your friend.) Or say you have a list of players and all you have is fax numbers. You have to generate pitch letters for each player and then fax out all the letters. Maybe you have a list of players and their e-mail addresses. You have to send each e-mail individually because you don't want to send one e-mail to ten players at the same time.

Sending out pitch letters is downright complicated and time-consuming. But it is doable. I started marketing my work when I was twenty, and it took me a while to get the hang of it. Over time you will learn tricks to make your job easier.

Test the Water

Once you have your database, have generated your letters for either mailing or faxing, and have prepared your e-mails, it's time to shop your script to Hollywood.

But wait a second.

Do you really want to send your pitch letter to every contact you have compiled in your database? You might want to test it first. Send it to twenty or thirty people—an equal mix of agents, managers, and producers. That way you can get an idea of whether your approach is effective. If you send out twenty or thirty letters and several people request your script, then you have a smokin' pitch letter. If no one requests your script, you might want to take a hard look at your pitch letter and make sure it's as strong as it should be.

Give the letter to a person you trust and tell them you're trying to create the illusion that you're a hot new writer and your script is the *next big thing*. Ask for feedback on the letter. Is it brief, and does it effectively sell you and your script?

The same effort that went into making your script wonderful needs to be spent on your pitch letter. This letter is your introduction to Hollywood. Make sure it's effective.

Once you test your pitch letter and know it's the best it can be, it's time to send it out far and wide.

Then the waiting begins.

What Happens When They Want You

If you send out a pitch letter and a player wants to read your script, he or she will usually get back to you quickly. Remember my pitch for *The Disposable Bride*? All the requests I received for the script came within two weeks. If Hollywood wants to read your script, you will receive calls, e-mails, or letters asking you to send it in.

Obviously, you need to have copies of your script and large envelopes, though if you're lucky, the person requesting your script will tell you to send it via e-mail. If you're asked to e-mail it, make sure you know what kind of document the person wants you to send (for example, a Microsoft Word document or rich text format).

However you send the script, make sure you include a very brief cover letter thanking the person for reading your material. I think it's helpful to include your logline in the cover letter. It reminds the person who is opening your package what your script is about. And don't forget to include your name and contact information

When mailing off your script, you might be tempted to send it to the player so they receive it as quickly as possible. Don't waste money sending your script via Federal Express,

UPS, or express mail. Your script won't get read any faster. Just send your package by regular first-class mail.

Also, if you are sending the script via snail mail, make sure to write REQUESTED MATERIAL ENCLOSED on the envelope.

Finally, some writers think you should send a self-addressed stamped envelope (SASE) along with your script and cover letter. An SASE is an envelope with enough postage on it that the person can return your script. I never include an SASE. For one, an SASE costs about the same as a copy of the script. Since I never send a used copy of a script out, it doesn't matter to me if I get it back. Secondly, my feeling is that including an SASE sends the wrong message, as if you're expecting rejection.

If the person reading the script wants to return it, great. If not, let them recycle it.

What Happens if No One Requests Your Script?

I have sent out pitch letters and gotten not a single bite. It happens.

Look at the bright side. At least you saved money on photocopies and postage!

Seriously, yeah, it hurts.

If you don't receive a response to your pitch letter, don't be discouraged. People in Hollywood are inundated with requests from writers to read their scripts. Thousands of people are trying to sell their scripts to the same people in Hollywood as you. There are only so many scripts these people can read.

If you send out a pitch letter and it gets *zilch*, take *another* look at it. Make sure it's the best it can be. Retool it. Heck, give your script a new title and come up with a snazzier logline.

Sometimes, though, no matter what you do, you won't get a request for your screenplay. That happened to me with *We Bitched!* and I was very surprised. I thought the title and concept were so cool.

No one agreed with me.

I finally just had to move on to another project.

Before you give up on a project, though, there might be something you can do to hustle up interest in your script. If you like to talk on the phone, you're in luck.

The Follow-up Call

Making follow-up phone calls after you send out a pitch letter can be very worthwhile.

A week or so after my partner and I sent out pitch letters for *Little Girls,* I phoned the office of an agent to whom I had sent a pitch letter. The agent's assistant picked up the phone. I explained that I was a new writer following up on a query.

The assistant couldn't recall seeing my letter. This happens a lot. Pitch letters are sucked into a vortex also known as the trash. Anyhow, the assistant asked me about the story. I gave her a very brief pitch about the script.

My partner and I signed with that agency very soon afterward. It never would have happened if I hadn't made that phone call.

Sometimes when you call players in Hollywood, it's difficult to get past the receptionist. If you *do* get through to a player's office, you probably won't get past the assistant.

This brings up a good point.

The assistant can be a wonderful ally for you in Hollywood.

Befriend the Assistant

Almost everyone in Hollywood has an assistant. Sometimes the assistants have assistants. No lie.

Nothing gets to an agent (or manager or producer or studio executive) unless the assistant wants it to. That means assistants are very important people to know in Hollywood.

Assistants are also usually ambitious people who want to be agents, managers, producers, or studio executives. They too are on the lookout for a new hot writer who has written the *next big thing.*

Cultivate friendships with assistants. They could help you get your script to the players.

Be Professional

One final thing about follow-ups. This is true whether you're following up on a pitch letter or a script.

Persistence *is* important in your screenwriting career. But there is a fine line between persistent and annoying.

Follow up on a pitch letter two weeks after you send it. If you're following up with a person who requested your script, give him or her about six weeks to read it. Then do your follow-up, either by phone or via e-mail.

Only follow up *once.* If you don't get a response to that one follow-up, you pretty much have your answer. The person you are trying to follow up with isn't interested in your pitch or your script.

Another thing. When you follow up by phone and are transferred to voice mail, don't leave a message. Your call will probably not be returned. Instead, try to follow up with the person later. Speak to them directly.

Above all, make sure you act professional on the phone. If you're young and don't have a lot of experience making business calls, work out what you want to say beforehand. If you make a call and manage to get someone on the phone and you freak out and tell him or her, "Oh my God, I'm so excited I'm talking to you, you just have to read my script, you just have to!" they will be like, *Click.*

Remember, to become a professional screenwriter (the one who cashes the fat checks) you have to act like a professional. No matter what your age. This goes for e-mail too. Keep your e-mails professional. That probably means avoiding the smiley faces (though I am kind of partial to them). :)

CHAPTER 5

That Elusive Million Dollars

You've probably figured out that writing a great script is not the key to making a million dollars. Making a million dollars involves writing a great script and successfully marketing it.

During your script-marketing journey, you will most likely be faced with a lot of rejection. When you are rejected, really what happens is . . . *nothing.*

No calls. No e-mails.

It's as if no one wants you.

When you're continually rejected, it's a slow, painful process that will probably make you feel frustrated, hurt, bitter, disgusted, damaged, depressed, angry, ugly, fat, and gross.

It might seem like a strange way to look at it, but rejection can be a friend if you know what you can gain from it. Rejection forces you to improve your script. Improve your pitch. Improve your marketing techniques.

Just keep improving. No one said this was going to happen overnight. Remember, thousands of people are trying to break into Hollywood as screenwriters.

Sometimes the writers who make it in Hollywood are the ones who face rejection year after year and still keep trying. They develop patience. Patience leads them to become very good rewriters.

Rewrite warriors.

Rewriting (your scripts and your pitch letters) is an important skill you will develop over time.

In this way, rejection *can* be your friend if it helps you become a better writer.

FINAL WORDS

Congratulations—You're a Screenwriter

As you near the end of the book, I want to say something unusual.

I want you to ignore my advice.

You already know how to write a script, you just didn't realize it. I've given you some nuts and bolts about what a screenplay is, but writing a screenplay is something you will figure out on your own. All you need to do now is believe that screenplay is in *you*. And write it, okay? Because you won't be able to bank a million bucks if you don't have a script to sell!

I said in the beginning of the book that selling a script will be difficult. It's a lot like playing the lottery. But it's very possible. I've seen people go from cashing unemployment checks to buying fancy cars.

Of course, the fat cash you can make writing scripts isn't a secret. Thousands of people know about it. Thousands of people are writing scripts. To make your million dollars, you have to be the one out of one thousand or more who is sold.

Your age is a valuable selling point. If you can write a

professional-quality script at a very young age, you have a strong chance of making money at your craft. Even if you don't make a million dollars, writing scripts will teach you important skills. And you might make money from other types of writing.

The first thing I ever sold as a writer was a book for young people. I wrote scripts for ten years (yes, a whole decade) and never made a dime. Then I wrote a kids' book and sold it nine months after I wrote it.

Selling a kids' book is no easier than selling a script. The money isn't as good, but it's still very competitive. Writing scripts, though, taught me all the skills I needed to make money at my craft. Screenwriting provides excellent training in becoming a good storyteller.

I just hope you know that you have very valuable stuff inside you. Your thoughts, emotions, and insights are astonishing. One day you may dazzle an audience with your brilliant story—as long as you believe that you have the creative ability to write it.

You do.

So I dare you.

I dare you to write FADE IN.

-THE END-

ACKNOWLEDGMENTS

Grateful acknowledgments to Paul, Laurel, and Jennifer, who had to deal with me on a daily basis during the writing of this book; to Carole, Cynthia, and my mom, Mary, who always provided necessary support to finish it; to all the people in "Hollywood" I've had the pleasure of working with over the years.

Finally, not enough thank-yous can be extended to Wendy Loggia and Beverly Horowitz for their support, enthusiasm, and guidance.

ABOUT THE AUTHOR

Colton Lawrence began writing at the age of nineteen and became a member playwright at the Group Repertory Theatre in North Hollywood. He spent many years in Hollywood developing his craft as a screenwriter and working with top names in the film and television business. He went on to write a unique how-to book in the voice of twelve-year-old Camy Baker, a book he self-published and later sold to Bantam Doubleday Dell. Four other Camy Baker books followed. He later cocreated and wrote the pilot episode for *The Deal with Jenny Shields*, a half-hour show developed at Fox Family Channel.